In Loving Memory of Shane.
Larger than life, even in death.

# THIS WAS NOT THE PLAN

*A Widow's Journey to Hope*

## BY: JENNIFER FARLEY

*jjpress*
LLC

This Was Not the Plan: A Widow's Journey to Hope

Published by JJOPRESS, LLC

© 2025 by Jennifer Farley

Printed in the United States.

Published 2025

ISBN 979-8-9993448-0-9 (Paperback)

ISBN 978-8-9993448-1-6 (Ebook)

# DEDICATION

To Tate, Lane, and Wyatt. May you always know how much your love helped me survive. May you always try and find the good in all situations, always be there for a friend in need, always know that love is worth it, always find contentment and not comparison, and may you always ride every wave of grief or happiness to its breaking point then hold on and ride it again.

# COVER ARTIST RECOGNITION

## Buddy's Masterpiece

Exploring the new pond was the first priority when we moved into our dream home. I stood behind the boys and took this picture of them admiring the spot where countless memories were made over the two years that followed. This photo was transformed into a painting that has been by our sides for over a decade.

Buddy Owens, the artist, was once Shane's roommate in Nashville, where they sang together as often as possible and worked part-time parking cars at the Loews Vanderbilt Hotel. Dreams explored and trails blazed. In 2000, Buddy began painting alongside fellow songwriter Ray Stephenson. His artwork can now be found featured in the homes of Carrie Underwood, Miranda Lambert, Easton Corbin, and many others. Our Lyle Lovett painting is a treasured piece, and the Nashville stories passed down by Shane are among our favorite memories. Buddy also painted the image on my Merle shirt mentioned later in the book. Buddy graciously offered to let me use our painting as the cover. There was no other appropriate choice. We love you, Buddy!

Buddy's songwriting credits include hits for Blake Shelton, Montgomery Gentry, and Mark Chesnutt, just to name a few. He also co-wrote a song with Owasso's own Nashville newcomer, Gracee Shriver. He's a hometown hero to us!

# Preface

I had friends who would not fly on the same plane as their husband on vacation, because if it were to crash, their children would have at least one parent left. Boy, they were really thinking ahead. This should probably be the norm, but typically, it is not. Maybe that seems extreme to you and you just want to live your life without constantly overthinking. You might even think that seems negative and you aren't trying to speak those kinds of morbid thoughts into your life. Maybe there's a middle ground? Are you never going to ride in the same vehicle?

Losing a spouse while having 3 young children is not something you plan for in your young, married life. Learning to roll with the post-loss punches becomes your daily mantra. Breathing, not for keeping a steady rhythm, but because each breath is necessary in sustaining your existence. Some days were, and often are still, like this. Talking myself into getting from point A to point B. The people who made surviving this possible are too numerous to mention but their care started day one. I didn't even blow dry my own hair for Shane's service…thanks, Lindsey!

My preacher, Blake, told a story about a little old man who was his neighbor dragging a hose out to water his trees. He would stand at the base of the tree. He wasn't watering from the top down. He was watering the roots. All good parents are giving their kids a strong and solid foundation from birth, even when the children are too young and not even developmentally ready to acknowledge this. I feel like my boys' roots were watered by their daddy. His caring, loving spirit nourished them. Despite his tough exterior, he showed them that it's ok to show compassion. It's also ok to be passionate about competing in life but you also need to be coachable. His musical talents taught them that if you have gifts, you should share them and it's ok to be creative and proud of it. His work ethic has continued to pay off in their dedication to what they feel strongly about and not one of them possesses an ounce of quit. It's just not going to happen.

This book is full of stories from the last decade. Thoughts, prose, and all of the divine intervention along the way. If you are a believer, read it. If you're a non-believer, read it. This book is for anyone who needs encouragement. If you know someone who has suffered a great loss, I hope to be a resource for them. My desire is realness, relatability, passion for friends and family, and the ultimate goal is to find hope. I have been in the trenches of hopelessness, loneliness, and desperation. No one should be there for long, and no one should ever go it alone.

# Table of Contents

# The Assignment

He didn't understand the assignment...he wasn't supposed to die.

The directions clearly stated forever.

Forever on this Earth isn't always possible, but 41 is too soon to go.

He didn't understand that the specific details were clear about the raising of children together - not apart.

He didn't understand that the three precious boys left behind with mom needed their dad.

They needed his jokes and jabs.

His guidance into their teens.

His wisdom as they found love.

He didn't understand that going meant his family shrunk exponentially.

He didn't understand the vastness of his very personality and presence.

He didn't understand grandchildren would eventually need to be enjoyed and then promptly sent home.

He didn't understand that once they were sent home, there would be me.

All to himself.

After all the years of marital, financial, and child-rearing trials.

He didn't understand that the aging process, while slow, yet fast at times, can also be quite beautiful.

He didn't understand that celebrating him without him here seems both a necessary honor and an emotional hardship.

He didn't understand the assignment.

WE THANKED JESUS FOR TAKING
GOOD CARE OF DADDY NOW.

# Dear Lady at Walmart,

7/6/15

I'm not sure I would consider you a friend. I may have shared a sideline with you once in a blue moon...on one team...6 years ago...when they didn't even keep score. Not that I am so competitive a person that the score matters, it's just a timeline reminder that you and I both have probably come a LONG way since.

If we talked on a daily basis, I may not have thought your line of questioning was rude. I may not have made a beeline to the other side of the giant store to avoid you or anyone remotely close to your demeanor. I may not have contemplated leaving my basket full of items and running for the hills. I was forced to stick it out with my sweet Wyatt and meander through the garden center...sweating and crying. My first trip to the store 'since' was becoming a joke...a bust.

You see, my amazing, handsome, strong, loving, hilarious husband left this world April 27, 2015. He was not supposed to go so soon.

My boys and I were not ready for him to leave. We have a lot of plans to fulfill...a lot.

So, lady at Walmart, you 'heard that we HAD to move?' Well, no. We didn't *have* to move. We chose to move from our 6 acres that we had just purchased not even 2 years prior. Many experts, and people who believe they are experts, say not to make such changes so suddenly. Although, when you watch your dear boys not be able to go into the room where daddy fell down and couldn't wake back up, you tend to consider it. When you have sat up on the couch one too many nights in a row just hoping that their brains are resting and not reliving the Monday over and over, you tend to entertain the idea of getting out of that house. I actually knew we could make it there, but honestly wanted a more manageable existence. We all 4 went and sat on our bedroom floor, right where it happened and prayed. We thanked Jesus for taking good care of daddy now. We prayed that our decision to sell was not about being scared, but about being smart. The first time that a volunteer didn't make their assigned mowing date and the grass was a little harrier than Shane or I would have liked it, I jumped on the tractor between school and practices and tried to knock out as much as I could. It was an emotional ride. Something that used to be my 'summer job' as Shane would jokingly say. What used to be a joy — me, my headphones, and my Colbie Caillat Pandora station — had become a chore. A teary, miserable reminder that he was gone and certainly not going to be sweeping in behind me with the weed eater to do the part of my summer job that I hated, all the while he would be teasing me from the ditch that I wasn't going to be on the American Idol tour any time soon. No, we didn't HAVE to move.

You asked, 'So where did you HAVE to go?' Well, lady now drawing a bit of a crowd at Walmart, since you asked like *that* I will tell you that not all widows are destitute, dumb, mindless, sewer dwellers who no longer seek what is best for their children. We didn't settle for a one bedroom apartment so that I didn't have to mow. We searched and found the greatest house that not only the boys would be proud of, but Shane would have totally lived in. He would not have loved the closeness of the neighbors, the 4th of July bicycle parade would have cracked him up, but I am CERTAIN he loves it for us! He has always been a tad bossy and such a leader. I have said more than once and completely believe that he is putting his two cents in with the man upstairs. Our home where we fully intended to host our grandchildren's summer camps sold in just 3 days. Multiple full price offers. Done. Sold. It had stayed on the market almost 2 years when we purchased it. Thank you, Jesus, for taking care of my sweet family. May the owners of that property enjoy the pond, the newly built barn where our middle son was going to raise baby lambs with my husband's help, where our oldest played on his own full-sized soccer field, and where our youngest learned a between the legs dribble on his own NBA court. When we prayed on our bedroom floor, my oldest asked that the new owners would know the love that was there. I will probably never remember that without crying. That is exactly what I want them to remember about that home. So, where did we *have* to go? Again, we didn't have to, but we chose to go somewhere manageable and safe. Somewhere that new memories could be made and the yard could get mowed. Co-dependent living is not something my husband would be proud of for us. He would be proud that I have accepted the help that I have, but I can mow my own yard. He would bear hug all of his buddies who have supported us and helped us move.

'So, like WHAT happened to him?' you so rudely continue to ask these pointed questions while cornering me on the chip aisle. We suspect he had a heart attack. 'What? You don't KNOW?' No, dear Lady, we don't. He was 41. He was diabetic. He chewed tobacco. He didn't always eat right. He exercised somewhat irregularly. He worked his tail end off for his family. He was probably too stressed. He coached a sport every season. He may not have had enough down time. He loved without ceasing. He made crude jokes. He popped me with towels in the kitchen. He teased his boys about girls and zits. He was a musician. He probably didn't get to play enough. He was the master of math homework. He drank beer on occasion. We traditionally both drank one when we grilled burgers on the back patio. He liked to play golf. He liked to watch college football, college softball, well...basically any sport. He loved his job. He was ornery. He was loved by everyone he met...even if he kept them guessing. He loved to go hunting with his work buddies. He loved a good surprise, even though he would tell you he didn't. He gave the best hugs. He loved me more than I have ever been loved. He always knew what to say to the boys. He was a born coach and encourager for kids. He loved his momma. He loved his daddy. His grandpa was his hero. He could roll with the punches. I could do this all day, but I didn't do this on the chip aisle. I had reached my limit with her in 3 questions. She wanted more, but I walked away. I hope she got the hint, but I am guessing not.

I have always been 'too nice'. My husband handled all buffering of uncomfortable situations. He could shut down a bugger in one word, one look, one movement. He hated going to the store with me since I had lived and taught in this town my whole life. It was too much. I have learned a lot about myself in the last 11 weeks. I am stronger than I thought I was and with divine intervention all around us, we will make it. My boys and I will keep moving forward, riding the waves of grief one day at a time. We will honor our memories and pray that new ones will become sweet again. We are not there yet. All of the sweet memories include dad. Right now, it feels like we are just moving through the daily motions. Staying busy and relying on family and friends to remind us that we are making it. We will continue to make it and continue to strive to honor God in all things. I will just avoid the chip aisle at all cost.

# Reactions Unknown

What to say? What to bring?

Maybe not a thing.

When to hug? When to cry?

Should I ask why?

How to feel?  They are no longer here.

I just want to be sincere.

It's the ballad of loss and friendship.

# Remembering Shane

## 7/6/2016

The decision was made by the boys and I to take Shane's ashes to Big Cedar. There are so many things to consider when you are doing such a thing. We went with the suggestion of a friend of ours who had just tenderly laid her parents to rest. A biodegradable urn that slowly releases the ashes to their final destination. A lake that meant so much to our family. A location unlike a cemetery, where many would go to mourn. This, and the fact that he wanted to be cremated, were two things I was happy we had discussed. He didn't like the expectation or obligation that people feel to go and visit a gravesite. I will never know if this was exactly what he had in mind, but I knew the cemetery wasn't it.

There were 27 of us. His family and mine. Together in our very favorite place to take the boys. The very place where he proposed. The very place we found out we were pregnant with Wyatt after believing we were done having children. The very place that will always be a part of our boys' childhoods and hopefully their family's future in the years to come. We had the best time and I know he is pleased and maybe a little shocked that we could all be together in our safe place. Our family is a tangled web…not a tree, but a flow chart with many sections, but love is there and support. That's what matters. The messy details didn't count this weekend.

Just a few short weeks before our celebration weekend, Shane's company honored him by dedicating the last tank he was in charge of to him. They didn't leave any stone unturned. We were flown there with two of the company representatives, one being Shane's best friend. Both men worked with him every day and were full of stories. He traveled often to Superior, Wisconsin to the tank fields there. We were fully outfitted in safety gear and they told us that Wyatt would be the youngest person to ever be let on site.

They drove us back into the facility, where there was a giant sheet magnetized to the side of a tank. They had a lift that a worker rode up on to reveal the large dedication guitar. It had the safety symbols that represented Shane's dedication to the project. At the bottom, there was his signature and life dates. The care and concern that his company showed the boys and me is unforgettable. The detailed drawing of a guitar underground with tree roots securing it was drawn by a man who worked alongside Shane when he would visit. It is the perfect representation of him, both at home and at work.

HE WAS RUNNING RIGHT
TOWARD THE ROAR...

# The Eyes Have It

7/22/17

When we dated, I knew I loved his eyes. I quickly realized they were identical to mine. Mine, my own eye color that had once led me to believe I had been adopted. The only one of my original, blood siblings without sea blue eyes and the only person I knew with hazel.

When he coached his very first team as a dad, a soccer team no doubt, we realized what came to be a very comical thing about those eyes. After a long season of YouTube tutorials and online soccer drill ideas, the football/baseball star was the Pirates' biggest fan and best leader. He had never played the sport that would become his oldest son's passion and reason for getting up every morning. The end-of-season party is one that we still talk about today. Shane leaned over to ask a little boy if he would like some ketchup on that victory hot dog he was about to consume and the sweet thing looked over his shoulder to see just exactly who Coach was talking to. Shane had a lazy eye.

After glasses with prisms so thick that you would have thought he was blind had been added to his weak prescription and many test runs to see if his diabetes was causing permanent retinal damage, it all came down to a tired muscle at the back of his eye. He became quite attached to his glasses. Never forgetting them for work meetings and always wearing shades when coaching.

He became quite accustomed to the jokes that followed. Most of the time, he made fun of himself. My brother liked to remind him that there is 'no lazy eye in team'. He would often make fun of the fact that he had been talking to someone and they didn't respond, saying, 'They didn't know who the hell I was talking to.' Our life was full of laughter and I know my kids learned that it is ok to laugh at your own shortcomings, but to love yourself all the same.

It was just two weeks after his passing that we got a letter from Life-Share stating that not just one, but two people had regained their sight with the help of Shane's corneas. I will never forget sitting in my driveway going through the mail and reading this. The boys had already gone in the house and I sat in my car, having hardly cracked a smile in weeks, and laughed until I cried. I then cried because I had laughed. The kind of emotional roller coaster that was best portrayed by the cast of Steel Magnolias post-funeral (another reason I knew I was supposed to marry Shane...his favorite movie). I was so over-whelmed with the fact that this had brought me nothing but joy that I had instant guilt, then realized that I would never see that green-eyed smile again in this lifetime, then started laughing all over again because of the irony of the eyes.

I calmed myself down and went into the house. I sat the boys down to read them the letter with a straight-face. As I calmly, carefully pro-nounced each word, I glanced up to see them fighting off the smiles. I kept reading and heard snickers from Wyatt and as I finished reading I saw Tate glance over at Lane and then they all erupted apologetically. Wyatt cautiously asked if the recipients would have lazy eyes as well. I explained that they would not, and admitted to sharing the same reaction in the car. I assured them that I knew we were indeed making their daddy so proud by our lighthearted approach to the news.

I have just today had the pleasure of hugging a daddy's neck who just lost his daughter. She has saved 5 lives so far through organ and tissue donations. While he cried, he told us just how excruciating this process has been and the varied emotions he has felt as the doctors planned and pieced his daughter's blessings to those who will continue to live because of her. He spoke of the private jet and limo rides for the families. He spoke of the babies, teenagers, and children who will no longer suffer because of her and how he had no doubt that they were getting the best and the strongest that this world has to offer. He was running right toward the roar today, as Levi Lusko speaks about in his book, 'Through the Eyes of a Lion'. Cueing the Eagle just like in Isaiah 40:31.

Through his inspiration, I was reminded that those hazel green eyes that I miss are right here with me. Three sets of them. Each of my boys share the same shade as their daddy and me. I am reminded that two people were gifted the view of life through his eyes. May they see things a little sassier than they ever dreamed they would, a little more vibrant, a little more loving, and a lot more focused.

# #saltlife
## (Now I Know What This Means)

7/30/2017

The counselor that I saw right after Shane passed asked if we had ever taken the boys to the beach. I told her we had always planned to. She requested that I take them in the next few summers. She said a beach vacation does something very different than any other...it slows you down. You don't have a thing to do but dig in the sand, listen to the waves, read a book, play, and just breathe. I remember her saying it resets your mind.

Yesterday, these boys were up at dawn after a late night and just sat on our balcony—unscheduled, unstructured, and staring out at the ocean talking to each other. I watched them play hard all day. They were so free. I thought about how lucky I am to be their mother and despite our cards being dealt, I never want to take that fact for granted...they are my gift. It was a short visit at the end of a long, fun week with our soccer family. I'm forever grateful that my sister, Ashley, will travel with me! It helps so much to not feel so overwhelmed and it's more love for my boys.

I know Shane is so proud of each of them. They are daring in their faith, love each other, and are such hard workers in all that they do! What a blessing the beach was!! If your family 'plans' to take a trip, DO IT! Save the money, make the time, because the saddest parts of my days are the things I wish we had done this side of Heaven.

MY HEART ACHES FOR MOMENTS WHEN
HE SHOULD BE HERE FOR THEM.

# Not Every Day is Pretty

8/23/17

I was recently reminded that I can't do it all. Who am I kidding...I get this reminder daily, but this was a biggy. Both of my older boys were sort of over me trying to convince them to shave with the electric neck trimmer that we use in between haircuts and probably embarrassed at the single blade Tinkle razor I told them to use on their little caterpillar stashes. They really needed to start the year with a fresh, real SHAVE. What's a mom to do?

I could have youtubed it, much like when we were trying to tie a bowtie for my niece's wedding but this was stressing me out just a little. I kept putting it off all summer and with just one day to spare, we had our shave lesson...compliments of Shane's best friend, Chris.

Much like he is with kids on the soccer or football field, he was patient and kind with just the right amount of 'just do it, you wussy'. I am not so sure that this wasn't a moment that Shane took over his vocabulary, but I am always mindful that they were around each other so much that they shared the same harassment tendencies.

Wyatt looked on with wonder. Lane kept a safe distance, but I could tell he was taking mental notes. Yes, he is a man-child. A new 13-year-old with more facial hair than his big brother. They have both had successful solo shaves and we are practically packing for college. It's a lot to take in.

After a week of school, I am finally writing about this because I have not looked at this picture without weeping since it happened. Shane should just be here. I know it's unfair for me to say that out loud, but it's the way I feel all of the time. The fact is, he's not. We are still learning to deal with that reality.

With each new school year, I feel more and more like I am on an island. I don't fit a lot of categories anymore. It's hard to have conversations with my married friends about the day-to- day and I certainly don't consider myself single. I have a hard time feeling sorry for people who consider themselves to be sooooo busy, and my compassion for everyday complaints is very minimal.

The only things I know are these:

I will continue to strive to be better, not bitter.

I love my job.

I care deeply for the students that God places in my care each year.

God is in control and I am not.

Some days are pretty good.

Some days are still not pretty at all.

I am in love with my boys and have no idea what I did to deserve them.

My heart aches for moments when he should be here for them.

I am and will always be eternally grateful for my true friends, coworkers, the boys' coaches and teachers, and for my family.

God doesn't expect us to put a nice face on an ugly thing, so I will work to continue to be honest in my feelings and keep living under His protection. Happy Shaving!

# Unkept Promises

Our vows were there and now they're gone. We weren't kidding with the whole 'until death do us part' bit.

What about the promises that we had for our boys? Teach them everything. Starting with tying shoes and only making it to a few seasons of ball seems like you chickened out on the rest.

I'm mad at times. I will just be honest.

Pissed.

Screaming at you from here.

I don't think there were even a handful of times that I was ever this mad at you.

My dad was supposed to be the only dad I was mad at. We agreed this wasn't going to be how our boys were raised…with only one of us.

Throwing the weed-eater across the yard like an Olympic track star throws the javelin wasn't something I had planned to add to my resume.

Your friends are great, but they aren't you. I can slowly learn to live but can these boys? Will they learn enough from me? Will they be wimps? I am very independent and have not had the easiest life overall. Grit. It's in me somewhere. Will this transfer? Like junior college credits becoming actual degree-earning credits?

Will I be enough to get them ready for life?

STRANGE THINGS HAPPEN AFTER LOSS.

# Sissy, No Bud...
# Monica, No Chandler

11/27/17

Here we are, year three of Christmas decorating...Joseph is still MIA.
When we unpacked our Christmas tubs after moving to our new
home, the boys and I went on a manhunt. We had not touched this
Christmas gear since last December in Skiatook. Why was he gone?
Ironically, we had been asking ourselves this since April when we lost
our leading man. Now, Mary is without, and life continues to be
severely unfair.

Strange things happen after loss. You feel like they are all happening
in slow motion. I remember asking the boys to help me look, as Mary
could not go on with just the camel, all three wise men, the cow, the
sheep, and no Joseph. She already had that whole virgin thing hanging
over her head, and so many haters were not seeing the big picture. We

looked in every dern plastic tub, even what I would have considered the 'junk drawer' of all tubs which had become my catch-all when we made the move. Shane had even repaired the angel's wing the year before; the slight overage of glue still visible. She made it in the designated Nativity tub.

But, no Joe!! Did Shane hide him? Will I see Joseph again this side of Heaven? Will I find him like I do other hilarious Shane objects around the house? An empty can of chew in his bedside table drawer (ew, but I am leaving it right there). Guitar picks. His tub of shoes that I cannot get rid of. His overalls in the closet. The doodles on my recipe cards from when he helped me cook Thanksgiving dinner several years in a row.

I recently decided that I was going to try to stop the spiraling thoughts that happen to me almost daily. I have asked the Lord to rebuke, remove, relieve, and denounce all of these irrational flashes from my very loud mind. This happens about 2 or 3 a.m. If I listed all of my worries anywhere but in my journal, I would likely be committed. Maybe we all would? I recently read John Green's new book. Much like every book I choose for pleasure, there are not one but two characters who have lost a parent. The young girl's father passed suddenly, her widowed mother is a teacher at her school (insert eye roll, head shake, or sweet warm fuzzy, you choose). This young lady has obsessive thoughts. He is such a genius writer. He quotes the greats at just the right times in a novel. 'In three words I can sum up everything I've learned about life: it goes on.' - Robert Frost.

I am slowly coming to grips with this. It does go on. It might be without Joseph, but it's not without Jesus. Wyatt loves to unpack baby Jesus. One year, he had been in a slight bit of trouble, and I saw him talking with baby Jesus at the Nativity about it. Precious! If we all could do the same. I find myself seeking His face more often than not. I need to see you in my life. I need a sign. A tangible reminder that there is more than worry here on Earth. I ask forgiveness for my selfish anxiety, but now realize that my body has had a real reaction to its current situation. My children are in the same boat. One more than the others. It is heart-wrenching as a parent not to be able to fix it. You want nothing more than to help them turn off their thoughts for just a moment. Anxiety is a real demon, and if you suffer, you are by no means alone.

So, as the season of hurry is now here. I vow to slow down my mind and body and enjoy my precious Nativity that was carefully chosen for Shane and me by a glorious couple in our church. It was a wedding gift in June of 2000 that has never meant more to me than it does now.

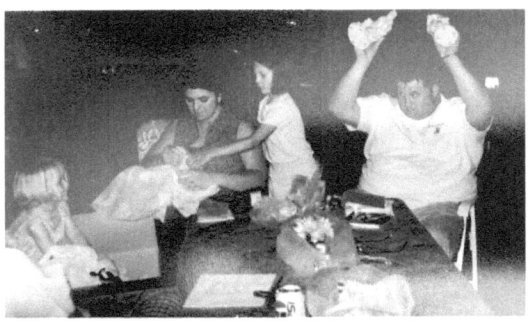

HAVE I EVER PUNCHED HER?
NO, BUT SHE WOULD TAKE IT!

# Do You Want to Punch Me?

## 1/31/18

My sister, Ashley, often asks me this very question. Like multiple times a week. Here's when:

- When we are at the salon and a sweet older gentleman is playing solitaire on his huge laptop while waiting for his dear wife to finish getting her nails done. He is carefully choosing each move, patiently waiting for her to be pampered.

- When running through Walmart to shop for classroom supplies, I stop in my tracks in front of the sporting goods because it seems like we were just there buying a fishing license.

- I take my oldest suit shopping and it doesn't go smoothly the first time. When we get home, he doesn't know what's wrong with him until we both realize we wish it wasn't just our job.

- When someone is griping about their sorry, no good husband for not helping them with something that seems suddenly trivial to me.

- When someone wants to get in an 'I'm so busy' contest with another mom in front of me, and I just sit and listen, trying not to laugh (or cry...scream, maybe).

- When my back door keeps sticking, and I fix it myself.

- When I have car trouble...even the slightest thing.

- When it's time for family or group pictures.

- When I have to tell a hostess how many to seat at a restaurant.

- When we are celebrating anniversaries.

- When my boys have a big win, and most kids are taking pics with the dads/coaches.

- When it's almost Valentine's day.

- When I have to call her for reinforcements after I found an old picture and immediately forget something I wanted to tell him.

- When I don't have the right advice to solve a boy problem.

I could do this all day, but I won't because Dolly said it best right after this scene...LAUGHTER THROUGH TEARS IS MY FAVORITE EMOTION. My sister knows how to break it down for me every single time. Have I ever punched her? No, but she would take it! We are in a lifelong recovery process that I know gets easier every day...then some days you feel like you took a giant leap back too many steps. We now know our way around things that trigger tough emotions, but it's the sneak attacks that are the hardest. My desire is to see the good in every season. To seek and find favor in the Lord's provisions. He is so faithful! To allow my boys to grieve naturally, and that it's perfectly healthy for them to see me struggle. I can't tell you how true this clip is for me. I have the GREATEST group of girlfriends anyone could ever ask for! They would each let me punch them square in the jaw if I needed to, and I can think of some men who would allow it as well! Thank you from the bottom of my broken heart for seeing the needs when they arise and being willing to be there in a moment's notice. My village is strong and mighty! We are blessed because of it!

# The 6th Grade Bully

My phone rang as I was dismissing my students.

'Your boy is running down 129th street!'

His best friend had called his own mom while running after him.

She was now calling me to let me know.

A bully had struck.

A hot-headed tween in his gym class…mad about being defeated during a routine game.

My sweet middle child, a gentle giant, had taken all he could when the boy crossed the line in the locker room and made fun of his daddy.

I can't even repeat what he said to him without tearing up, but it was an instant heartbreaker.

My precious boy shoved him. Hard.

Reflex, reaction, instinct, or boiling point?

He then ran to be alone. He ran until he came to a safe place. His best friend, leaving school too, to track him and be there when he stopped.

Protection and solace. Fear and frustration.

Bullies are cowards.

# Is He Proud of Me?

4/4/2018

3 - That is the number of days that my boys had insurance after my husband suddenly passed away on April 27, 2015. His gracious company wanted so badly to extend the time but he was 'no longer employed' through them, so by law...they couldn't. They verbally committed to helping me if any need for healthcare should arise until I could get it handled.

Get it handled? I was handling a lot of things I didn't want to be handling. When I called Mrs. Carpenter at the Administration building to discuss my options, I found that there were none I could afford. She very gently and sweetly told me to consider SoonerCare for my boys. My first reaction was, "WHAT? No I am an educated woman with a career. I should be able to take care of my children's insurance needs."

$8,000.00 - That was the amount of usable, bring-home income that

I would be lacking every month without him. Yes, he had worked his whole life from 14 to 41, so the boys would be getting some survivor benefits through Social Security. However, those weren't enough to get the insurance. Those are barely enough, combined with my teaching salary, to feed everyone, maintain their activities, and carry on their life somewhat as they once knew it.

SoonerCare: It has been a blessing and a curse. I remember sending my boys back to school just a week after losing Shane and feeling a real urgency to stay close to their buildings that day in case they needed me. I hid in my sister's office, and she and I literally prayed over her computer as I hit submit on the SoonerCare forms online. I cried tears of joy when I saw that they were approved. I cried out of shock that it was that easy to prove my case for assistance. I printed their temporary insurance cards and began a life of assumptions at the doctors, pharmacies, dentist, and optometrist. Once, when checking in at the doctor, the receptionist said snidely about some needed paperwork, "Oooooh, you're on SoonerCare." I had frankly had enough of the shameful comments and haughty glares and plainly told her that, yes, because my husband is dead and I'm a public school teacher.

You see, what I really wanted to say was…Yes, I have government-assisted healthcare for my children because my children mean more to me than my pride. Yes, I have a career and a 4-year-plus degree. Yes, I wish my profession thought enough of my family to offer better pay and comprehensive insurance options. And no, I am not working the system. Every year, when I reapply and I get approval, it will continue to be a blessing until it's not. Then, I will seek counsel and possibly look to another state or industry for work. My boys have had enough change to deal with in one lifetime, so I would like to avoid this option. Financial security can be a very taxing reality once it is gone.

I submitted the above as a part of my Teacher of the Year portfolio. I sent it to lawmakers. It is raw, honest, and EMBARRASSING. I have been feeling like I should share it to throw a little perspective to some. I am not looking for sympathy and really don't want to be treated like the second-class citizen that I have occasionally been made to feel like for having to take advantage of such a program.

One sweet friend assured me that my situation is why Soonercare and programs like it were originally put into place. For people who have life hand them an unfair slap, not for people who don't feel like working. I work. I will continue to work. I WANT to take care of my kids. It's my solo job now, and I take it very seriously.

I often wonder what Shane is thinking about all of this. We had many discussions about my job, and he KNEW I didn't do it for the money. He loved my breakdown of the day at dinnertime, and he became invested in the lives of my students. Would he be proud of Oklahoma educators? I have NO DOUBT he would! First and foremost, he would not want me to feel embarrassed for trying to continue the life that I loved and for providing for our boys. I know it's not right to worry, so here I am trying to gather my prayer warriors once more to get us through the day.

I AM REMINDED HOW MUCH BIGGER GOD
IS THAN ANY OF MY QUESTIONS.

# And All That It Implies

5/13/18

Here it is, my view on Mother's Day morning. I am having my coffee and sobbing. I can't quit. This day tears me up every year. Since becoming a mother, it always has. It has nothing to do with my own mother. She is great and deserves a parade in her honor. She single-handedly raised four kids who are now successful adults. We used to even celebrate her on Father's Day. She was just that good! A survival parenting style that left us all tougher around the edges than we may even need to be. We will celebrate her today!

This day is heart-wrenching now because I can't go to church and lean into my husband's strong shoulder and cry while we worship. I can, on the other hand, have my coffee and stare at the very gift he gave me when Tate wasn't quite one. On my first Mother's Day, he gave me this birdbath. I will cherish it forever.

Why all the tears? I am a blessed momma of 3 magnificent beings—three boys who would do anything for me. Three boys who are respectful and kind, whom I now lean on for strength, and whom I pray over and ask for guidance to try and make them the best they can be.

I cry for my friend who never knew his mom as anything but an addict. For my friend's girls who are without her today because she took her own life. For the teenage mom we know who wasn't sure what to do and gave her baby up for a better life for the child. I weep for my friend who lost her mom to cancer, and my other friend whose mom is losing her battle now. For the mom and dad who made the decision to donate their dying child's organs for another family to have life. For all the confused students I have had over the years who haven't known the kind of mother who I feel they should. For my stepmom, my dad's third wife, who has kept my dad sober for decades, and for my half-siblings whom I wish I could see more often.

Shane and I both had moms who had been through their own loss—husbands who decided that another woman was better. I now have many friends who have gone through the same experience, leaving them with no husband to help celebrate them today! Cherishing even the smallest gesture of acknowledgment from their kiddos on a day like today. For these women who put on a brave face at every ballgame, every parent-teacher night, every family function alone...you didn't ask for this and you are better than you will ever think you are! Do not let it define you or make you bitter. There are men out there in this same situation, and I applaud the ones I know who are killing this mom job! We have two in our family. They are there for their kids every day, without fail.

When Shane and I told his dad and his dad's wife that we were expecting, we were so very excited to take them to dinner and let them know. They were not outwardly excited, and we later found out that it was because they were trying to conceive and had bad news along the way. A baby lost. We had no idea. They then had success and my sweet brother-in-law was born just 4 months after Tate. Motherhood is a battle that some have to fight harder to be a part of than others. It is a miracle.

My sister was pregnant when I was expecting Wyatt. We were going to have babies at the same time!!! She lost her babies, four in total. Why is this even a thing? Why are mothers teased in this way? Why is it that my brother and I were blessed with these perfect babies and our two sisters can't have that same maternal gift? I have a lot of questions surrounding this, and then I am reminded how much bigger God is than any of my questions.

My oldest sister told me once, about a year after we lost Shane, that she was at peace with no longer putting her body through the abuse of trying to conceive. She felt at peace, knowing that God had given her so many of her own miraculous opportunities here. First, her stepchildren. She is their S'mommy and has done a darn good job of raising them as her very own. They are adults now, and she felt that God knew I would need her. She is my extra set of wheels to deliver children, my extra set of brains when mine is in a fog of grief, and my extra set of ears when the boys seem down or when I need to vent. She rescues me. Often! And, selfless is her middle name.

I feel for my own mother-in-law, who wishes to get one more hug from her son today. One more teasing remark about how she would like him to help her do some 'moving things around' for Mother's Day. I remember one year she wanted a bench for her backyard. We spent hours at the statuary shop in Skiatook with her. Trying to be patient, as she hadn't just picked out a bench, but many other very heavy items that he had to deliver back to her house and set up for her. I can hear his choice words now...but he would have done it again and again.

So, can we simply celebrate this as a beautiful Sunday? Another day that the Lord has made for us to enjoy. That's what we will do! Moms, Stepmoms, Girlfriends helping raise little ones, Dads doing mom jobs, ex-wives, new wives, aunts, uncles, moms and grandmas in Heaven, teachers influencing and loving on kids who don't feel that love at home, pastors who are trying to say the right things this morning, moms with graduates, perfectly traditional family units, moms with military children, moms of fur babies, dads who stepped up for someone else's children, coaches who love kids unconditionally, neighbors who bless others...have the best day you can!! Enjoy the blessings from every angle! Embrace your family tree, flow chart, bullet point list, or multi-level pyramid that may at times seem like a scam. Own your dysfunction. Love on those God gave you and those he took too soon. Happy Mother's Day, and all that that implies.

I WILL BRING THE BLANKETS
AND STAND WATCH.

# The Navigation of Grief

8/2/18

So many things come to mind when someone asks me how my summer is going. I want to say it's good. We have spent some time relaxing, which we actually stink at, and some time doing our typical summer 'list of things you can't get accomplished during the school year'. It has been enlightening. My boys are growing up. I am their cruise director, their camp counselor, their principal, their mechanic, and sometimes we are friends. There is an important balance to consider with teens and a 10-year-old. They are amazing humans, and they are my purpose. They are learning to live again with no reservations, and they are reaching high for goals that even the most traditional of family units would think were lofty. They complete me.

I have had a few things on my mind. The unthinkable happened, and another precious man left the Earth too soon. This event marks the second of Tate's teammates who has lost their dad since we lost Shane.

I had the pleasure of teaching 2/3 of this sweet man's children and getting to visit occasionally with him and his wife at soccer games. He was a rare jewel, full of compliments toward his children's teachers and coaches. Always put a smile on my face. After attending the service with my oldest and standing off to the side with him when it was over, I realized what he was doing. He was watching his teammate and just patiently waiting. Waiting to see if he would need him. When the crowd began to clear, I could see his friend slowly eyeing Tate to make sure he was still there. No words exchanged. He waded through the last few people in the crowd and came straight to Tate, giving him a hug, and then it was time to go. It was a long time. Much longer than my son realized. So long, that the funeral director, a friend of mine and the same person who had handled Shane's service, came and whispered, 'You know it's over, right?' He's a joker. I imagine a sense of humor is mandatory in that line of work.

I have since reached out to the grieving widow. I have been able to help with things that other people would not talk about over coffee. Death certificates, etc. It has been both therapeutic and awful. It was the moment when I told her that nothing would seem strange to me if it helped her heal...I knew I was healing as well. You want to sleep by your man at the cemetery? I will bring the blankets and stand watch. You want to scream and cry and tell me it's not fair? I will agree and get you some boxing gloves. You want to relive your first date? I will set the table. You want to type a blog post at 5 am in his softest, most favorite green t-shirt that has been cried into many, many times when you can't sleep? Let's do this! Most importantly, I will pray for your family—every single day.

Tate added the song that they played at the service to one of our play-lists. I listen to it every time I go for a walk and pray. Often through tears, I ask the Lord to protect that family as He has mine. To surround them with people who genuinely care and have no expectations for their process. To allow them to embrace life in a way that their man would have wanted them to. I often realize that my prayers are for my family as well. We no longer know how to celebrate. We struggle through birthdays and some holidays. Everything could just be so much funnier, happier, sillier, more carefree if he were here. Games would be more exciting, and trophies and medals would be more appreciated. Easier. Yes, easier for me and my boys. Sunsets would be more beautiful, flowers would smell better...you get my point?! We are still learning.

Part of my learning to cope has been to write when my thoughts get too loud. I was gifted a new traveler's notebook from my school last year as part of my Teacher of the Year award. Some people choose jewelry, and I decided on more school supplies. Ha! I'm super fancy like that. Honestly, it is deliciously leathery and beautiful! I am in love with the way it opens and the paper inside. I am a total nerd and proud of it. It has helped me through some rough times to write with a purpose. To list out troubles, only to find them heavier in ink than in thought. Most of the time, they are minor. If something that seems so small can help me, maybe it can help you too. I have also taken opportunities as they come to me with my friends. I attended a Christmas party this year for the first time in five years. Yes, I had four events in a row this week on my 'social' calendar. I only made one of them, and I was late, but hey, I went to one! I didn't skip because I wanted to; it took two other adults for me to make the one that I did. Three kids in sports is no joke, and I would rather be with them. Someone said that you only get 18 summers with your kids, so make them count! Ugh! Sad!

Part of navigating grief is making some split-second decisions that you would never have thought were important before this journey. Things that seem simple to some people. Introductions. The one event

I made it to this week was our new Book Club!! Super fun and right up nerd alley for me. An exciting new tribe of readers!! But how do I introduce myself to a group of ladies, half of whom I do not yet know? Is it better to say: Hi, I'm Jen. I have three fabulous boys, I lost my husband suddenly three years ago, I enjoy gardening and decoupage, travel and long walks. OR Hi, I'm Jen, I have three fabulous boys who are the light of my life and now let me ramble on about how amazing they are because I am super good at that!

I chose option 2. The trouble with that option is that at our next meeting, someone will casually ask where my husband works or something equivalent. I will then have to make them feel uncomfortable by saying that he passed away. There will then be side eyes as that person tells her friend who she is closest to and so on so that they won't be in the same position. It is all very understandable, yet I am unsure which is worse for those around me.

There are also problems with option 1. Talk about putting a damper on the evening. Some people just can't. It negates anything that anyone else says in an introduction. It's oddly show-stopping. I just can't.

This is not reserved only for book clubs. This is every new season of sports, every new school year, and new teachers, every new class that I teach, every new friend that I make. I am pleased to say that I recently filled out some forms without tears. I can now check boxes and complete enrollments without breaking down. I've almost gotten talking about it with my students down to an art. Seventh graders want to know your life story, so it's going to come up!

I want to make it a meaningful topic, and that's hard to do on the spot. So maybe introductions come with time as well? For now, I will do my best at making that decision on the spot and depending on the circumstance. I will keep journaling and keep praying! I read a book this summer by Rachel Hollis, and my takeaway from her is that you can only really control two things: Your attitude and your effort. So I will continue to try and keep both of those things positive and centered in Christ.

CONTENTMENT IS A HARD CONCEPT
WHEN YOU LOSE SOMEONE.

# More Please

8/27/18

**More...**

- anniversaries, at least 30 or so

- birthday parties planned and executed with probably more flair than necessary

- friends over for dinner and fishing

- fight nights where the girls never even know the fight is on

- date nights to buy every Christmas gift on the boys' lists in one night

- being teased about basically everything

- vacations...lots more

- problems solved together

- advice given to our boys that only a dad can deliver with such certainty

**Many more...**

- plans for retirement RVing to every Bluegrass festival we could find

- teams to coach

- boats to captain

- eye rolls when I had a new project in mind or it was my turn to host bunco, which were basically one in the same

- conversations about our work days over an early dinner before leaving for practices

- weddings to attend where he was singing

- ballgames where we sat apart because of his 'passion'

- plans to be the coolest grandparents someday

- plans to never be apart so our kids wouldn't have to know what that feels like

**Man, what I wouldn't give for more...**

- laughs

- inside jokes

- looks

- trips around the dance floor

- memories

- hugs...bear hugs

- encouragement

- unconditional love

Three years gone is too long to still have a lifetime of unfulfilled plans. Contentment is a complex concept when you lose someone. I am always praying this over my boys. For them to find peace. I don't allow myself to go through this list often, but I did write it down, and it sums up a tiny fraction of what I'm missing without him. I could add details daily.

Three was our signature number. We dated three times, therefore chose June 3rd as our wedding date, and we went on to have three boys, basically three years apart...Wyatt being a bit of surprise. So, I think I knew this year's date would be challenging. I have come farther than to try and think it isn't my life now. It is. But I will allow myself to wish for things today that I do not have. I don't feel like this makes me a bitter person. I am not. I have accepted that it makes me normal. I am human. I can occasionally yell. "This is NOT FAIR!" because, frankly, it isn't. I can't stay there. I am living daily under the protection of my Savior. There is no other explanation for how we get from point A to point B.

I couldn't be more proud of my boys and who they are becoming. Tate had an assignment in his psychology class and he texted me to ask what a stressful event was for him in the last few months. Neither of us could think of anything. We were naming the most random things that to some people would have seemed huge. I texted him back and said...I think our definition of stress is so different from some people's. His words were, "I know, Mom, everything seems minor." I am sorry they know this truth due to something so unthinkable. I am glad they are warriors. They make me stronger.

God's got this! The THIRD chapter of Ephesians even says that God has more in store for us than we can even imagine. Thank you for your promises! They cover and carry me.

IT'S THE EVERYDAY STING
THAT I WISH WOULD GO AWAY.

# Donuts with Dads

10/24/18

Yesterday was a professional development day for the teachers in our district. My sister and I taught something 'google-y' as we tend to do. It's fun and usually well-received by our peers. It's practical information that I pray teachers will use as soon as they get back to class today. Some of these days are spent by teachers grumbling about needing to attend any type of continuing education. I agree we have had some dud days but I appreciated the choices we had yesterday.

Since losing Shane, I have had at least one student (this year two) gifted to me who has lost a parent. I say gifted, because that is the way I feel about every child who is in my class. They are a gift, and they are there for a reason. Because of this and other obvious reasons, I chose a class about grief. I remember the first year after loss that I had a grieving student who was pushing every limit. Late to class, not doing his work...a brilliant little guy, but he was using his loss as an excuse. I took him into the hallway and had a little tough-love conversation with him. I reminded him that I had dropped off three boys just like him that morning, who I expected to be sad at times, but never disrespectful of the rules. That it would eventually make more worry for his mother if he didn't straighten up. I remember crying with him and telling him I understood, but to a point. I wanted so badly to know that I had said all of the right things. I called his mom and told her about our conversation, and she was grateful. She told me that sometimes it takes someone else telling him.

I agree with that! Tate would not eat, and I called in reinforcements. A hip, amazing young dietitian who was also a lover of running. She gave him the same calories-in/calories-out talk that I had, but he is still abiding by her advice today. Lane thought a rule was far-fetched, and it took our family friend Chris to help him see the light. Sometimes one parent gets to play off the other in the whole good cop/bad cop scenario. Well, when there is only one, you need to have backup. Chris coincidentally had to be called off duty when another parent questioned my parenting decisions. Stand down, friend. They've definitely got my back! Just like Shane would have expected them to!

I wanted this professional development to help me see a different side of the few kids a year that I have who are grieving. I am so close to this at home and often worry about what my boys look like in a classroom setting. Are they focused? Are their thoughts drifting? Do they feel scared, helpless, alone? I am just naming off all of my own daily feelings here. They can be miserable.

Here are my takeaways, and they apply to anyone who desires to understand better a friend or family member grieving:

- 1 in 20 children will deal with a death loss by age 7, and many more are dealing with a life loss. There is a difference.

- Life loss is when their mom/dad might be out there, but chooses a different life. I find this very sad and a whole other blog post. This scenario was about me growing up...do they love me? Why are they choosing another family?

- Children dealing with the loss of a parent do not trust everyone around them to still be there in the future. That could have been said for anyone, but can you imagine their uncertainty?

- Kids tend to grieve in bursts. Don't be surprised if they are ready to face the world moments after an outcry.

- Children of loss deal with new aspects developmentally. For example, a 3-year-old who loses a parent may ask the living parent DAILY where that person is. When that same child is 5 or 6, it becomes concrete that they are not coming back. When they are 10, they learn there is evil in the world, and they may suffer all over again with other worries associated with death. Coincidentally, this is where I am with Wyatt. Bad dreams, locking the doors excessively...I mean, who wasn't afraid to take the trash out in the dark at some point in your childhood? It's all normal, but may be escalated for these children.

- They could relive the death at every significant life event. Wishing they were there for all of the big moments. The big game...the concert. What is graduation going to feel like? Leaving for college?

- It is essential for everyone to know: not one single thing you do or say can take away someone's grief experience. Just sit with them, don't tell them 'it will be ok', or other ridiculous things we all say because to them it just won't be, and just be still. Help them normalize their feelings so they don't think they are going crazy.

The reason for the title of this post is that Donuts with Dads came up...why do we do these types of things? Well, because the majority of the population can enjoy it, while others are forced to face their grief head-on. Rewind to my first DWD experience as an elementary teacher, and you will know that I have been bitter about it from day one. We had a student whose father didn't show. They were supposed to meet them there. It was a day ruined for this child. They will likely never forget it. The counselor explained yesterday that we can't shield them from every hurt and if it gives them a chance to unpack some feelings, then so be it. I agree. I can't believe I'm agreeing, but I do.

It's the everyday sting that I wish would go away. My boys have had things bother them that I wouldn't have dreamed would, but each time it's been a chance to talk. To cry. To let it out! I didn't even make it through senior night at the football game, thinking about next year for Tate. I'm going to require some mighty prayer warriors for all of these life events!

Something I am very grateful for is Wyatt's lunch bunch. He participates in this at school with his counselor and other children dealing with a loss of any kind. What I believe is the key is this, they just eat lunch. They play and act silly. They visit about nothing in particular, but they start each time with their club rules, and the one that sticks with Wyatt is: Whatever happened to create this loss was not my fault.

# Perfect Parents

Are there such things as perfect parents?

Does any child think this exists?

I would love to be the perfect parent, yet I am finding it difficult as a solo act.

A constant monologue as the protagonist…missing an antagonist.

Possibly the other way around, but you were a softy.

I assume many traditional parenting duos feel much the same if there isn't support from their spouse in discipline and daily handlings.

It's a real shame, but I accept the challenge with the help of others around me.

Lord, help me. I beg you to bring things to light that need addressed if I miss something.

I want them to have the best chance at a full and successful life.

I want them to feel supported and accepted.

WE ALL GRIEVE DIFFERENTLY, AND
NONE OF US ARE PERFECT PARENTS!

# Thanks Be!

11/20/18

An opportunity to share comes along once in a while, mostly just with my students or a friend who is hurting. A year ago, my longtime friend Londa asked me to speak at a women's event at her church. I suppose for a solid year I pictured a fellowship hall with some donuts and maybe 50 ladies, half of whom I was related to or had worked with.

Fast forward to a chilly Thursday evening in November, 320+ women gathered in a lovely sanctuary filled with the most amazing fall décor, as if Joanna Gaines had been there. A meal was shared, games and door prizes were offered, worship took place, and the night was one I won't soon forget.

When you step on stage with that many faces staring back at you, you quickly realize you may just be better at the written word than the spoken. I could feel the prayers of my many friends who knew just how real I wanted to be. The devil had tried to convince me a few weeks before that I was not worthy to be in front of a group. He didn't win, and I am not perfect, but God gave me a story to tell. It's not a pretty one, but I got through it.

Londa and I had spoken after Shane's service about practical ways the church can better serve a widow or widower from the very start, and she decided she would like for all women to hear about it at the event. I tried to unveil the reality of my ups and downs with the process so far. I do not mince words with God. He knows how much I have hated many things that have happened, but if I could help even one lady to see that it is possible to survive even the unthinkable, then it was worth it!

I had the opportunity to tell about the most horrific night of my life, and I had rehearsed it in my head so many times that it went reasonably well. What I had not prepared myself for was walking into the same sanctuary that we used for Shane's service. It was graciously offered to us by First Baptist Owasso because we attend Life Church and we were not sure there would be room. We packed the place on that beautiful Spring day. I walked in to find my seat that evening and was punched right in the gut with those undeniable feelings of grief. I could picture the boys and me walking across the front. I went back into the hallway, and my phone was ringing. It was my friend Lindsey who assured me that she was praying and might be a little late, but she would be there. Perfect timing. I told her what was happening and was able to talk through it with her.

It was my turn. Londa asked me some questions after I shared the initial reason I was qualified to be there as a woman who had survived trauma. There was laughter, a fist pump from Sarah at the back of the room that I could see from the stage, and there was another table of my family right up front. I know that Shane was honored, and the reality of life as a solo parent was brought to light. My biggest advice: DON'T JUDGE. We all grieve differently, and none of us are perfect parents! Be there for people no matter what they are going through. Be still. Listen. Offer a kind word through text when someone falls on your heart.

One of the other women who spoke talked about keeping your circle small. I almost thought that was contradictory at first, considering we were in a room of hundreds of women, but I GET IT!! I have had a few hard relationship realizations since losing Shane. Some people want to keep you close to know your business, and not because they want to help you. It's ok to be choosy. I loved the whole thing! I would do it again. I even had more to say, but I believe I am a little more organized in my written thoughts. In the words of the iconic Led Zeppelin, I fear I will ramble on without written guidelines.

Since then, I have had so many questions about my notebooks. I carried them with me like a security blanket. They are dear to my heart, as they hold many secrets! They keep me organized and sane.

**The products I love:**

**Chic Sparrow** - My delicious Mr. Darcy in Buttered Rum. He has been a true friend in times of trouble and inspired moments. The leather is divine!! I can't thank my friend Jenny enough for introducing this company to me! She's a devoted customer and does the coolest things. She keeps several notebooks for a various reasons. For instance, she keeps a quick daily diary for her son to have when he's grown, tucked away in one of their smaller notebooks. The sizes and insert descriptions can be found on their website.

**May Designs -** I have thoroughly enjoyed this site for many years. Again, my paper-loving friend, Jenny, got me my first May Book ever for Christmas one year. I enjoy so many things, but mostly the easy customization of these beauties!! I LOVE the Prayer and Gratitude Journal, the calendar choices, and a notebook with dotted pages and graph-lined pages. Y'all, I love them all!! There are so many other great gift ideas, from pregnancy journals to meal planners. My favorite is the quality and design choices (even for the Holidays)! This company has been featured on Good Morning America, in Real Simple, and is in Birch Boxes nationwide, as well as one of Oprah's Favorite Things!!! *'It makes my heart happy that some simple little notebooks helped you through some difficult times.'* -Mica May, CEO

**Little Mountain Bindery -** I am a little newer to the LMB fan club. My LMB was the one I was gifted from school. It is yummy!! The soft leather and beautiful details are rich. I love that it's made right across the Okie border in Arkansas. A small bindery that repairs bibles and vintage books. I have the Classic Brown Fillion with a red cord. *'It makes me so happy to hear that you love your Fillion and that it helps you in day-to-day life.'* - Lesha Shaver

Ok, I was FANGIRLING over and over receiving these emails! I always tell my students never to be afraid to tell someone how much they love a product! We need to appreciate the businesses that make us happy and more efficient citizens. My heart is a little fuller this Thanksgiving, and I know Shane is grinning from ear to ear in delight at my joy!

HOW DO I KNOW THAT HIS LIFE
STILL MAKES A DIFFERENCE?

# Warning Bell, The Wonder of a Legacy

1/13/19

My little sister reached out to me in July of 2017 and told me to listen to this guy, Ryan Montbleau, and tell her it doesn't sound like Shane. She said she had this one particular song on repeat for the last week. I urge you all to listen and tell me it's not true. I emailed the artist the very next day and explained my situation...that my husband's voice was sprinkled in his like the best seasoning you could ever add to a dish. He wrote me back, thanked me for reaching out, and told me to let him know if the boys and I ever needed anything. He's still one of our favorites!

He writes about strangers telling him he isn't ready, and that he has miles to go in life. He asks how many people who have passed were actually ready? How many got a warning? Felt it coming? Did any of them hear a shot of the warning bell?

I will never know if Shane felt ready or felt a warning in his soul. I vividly remember working in the garden the very week before and talking about how he would go before me. He was mostly joking, but was he feeling something? My heart tells me maybe he was.

How do I know that his life still makes a difference? When people assure me that my boys are doing great. When I see a little Shane in their decisions...whether that is an ornery one or a great one. When I look at the life we built in almost 15 years of marriage and realize how much we've experienced together. It's really hard when you can't talk to someone you're used to talking to any time to see how they think things are going. I wish that not only could I feel reassurance in the wreck of decisions that have come my way since losing him, but I so desperately want my boys to know their dad as I did. Someone with a heart of giving. Someone who spoke his mind in love and loved deeply. Someone loyal. Someone who wasn't done making a difference and wanted to leave a mark for them to follow.

Well, last week, a sweet lady called from LifeShare. Vicki has been with me for a while now. She knows that while some people don't want or need to know every detail, I do. I have asked where every part of Shane has gone. She will read me a list any time I want to hear it. Everything from 2 adults regaining their sight, to multiple skin grafts for burn victims. She explained to me that not many tissue recipients reach out to donors, but that if we ever receive a letter, she would let me know right away.

We got a letter. All we know is the man's first name. I get it. He has no idea who we are, but he had the tender compassion to reach out and help us heal. If I could write him back, this is how it would go.

Steve,

We love you for letting us know Shane's impact on your life. I am so proud to know that you are a lifelong athlete. I am raising three amazing athletes myself. Shane was an athlete and one of the best coaches I've ever seen. The kids loved him! He was tough, but they knew he loved them back. While we don't know which college or professional team you were a part of, we are most excited that your spinal fusion was a success and that a little part of Shane can now help you continue an active, healthy lifestyle.

I am most excited that you find a true blessing in now being able to play with your little granddaughter. She will never forget it! Shane was a baby magnet, and we had just purchased our forever home where we had many back porch chats about how our grandchildren would run and play on the land. He would teach them to fish and appreciate a beautiful sunrise and a sky full of stars. Please think of him if you get the chance to do these things with her.

May your family know how much your letter has helped us and will continue to impact the stories my boys will tell about their dad for the rest of their lives.

Much love,
The Farley Family

If you had a warning, would you change anything? I have learned a great deal in this process, but most of all, that the power of our impact on those around us is priceless. Shane is still impacting others! Thank you, sweet Savior, for the gift of music, for the gift of this letter, and for having our backs every day!

GRIEF IS NOT THIS SIMPLE.

# Grief's Broken Compass

1/23/19

Nothing will make you more grateful for technology than a teen driver in your family. From plugging in an address to maps to tracking their locations, mom is just a call away while sitting still in a safe, well-lit location, of course. Grief is not this simple. If I could find a magic piece of technology to show me the way, my last several years would have gone much more smoothly. You see, my husband is gone, my boys are staggering at times, and my compass has just been spinning.

Shane was the most hilarious part of my day. He was the coach of all coaches for each of the boys' endeavors, an actual kid magnet, the fixer of all wrongs, the less serious of the pair of us, and our very fearless family leader. He passed away on a rainy night in April of 2015, and the truth for us in feeling lost is that I was usually the driver if we were in a hurry. He refused to drive over the speed limit, but he was always the designated navigator. We made an amazing team on our travels through the day-to-day!

We have three handsome little men that are mine to raise. How am I supposed to know how to do all of this? The first answer is that I, alone, am not. The number one best decision I have made in this journey has been accepting help. My family, all of whom are not blood related, have saved me from many a mom blunder. I sent my youngest son's skating money and bingo basket money yesterday in an envelope that I found on the floorboard of my car with no forms attached, just some chicken scratch in a pink marker that also happened to be in the car. I emailed the teacher and apologized later. I once called a friend while at a wrestling tournament and asked her to completely outfit my oldest in one of her husband's suit coats and a tie because I had no idea that the dinner he'd been invited to required a jacket and I was 45 minutes away. My sister has dedicated the last few years of her life to as many practices, games, and state-to-state travel as I have. I want to say I'm better than all of that, but the real answer is that I want my boys to still experience everything that is part of being a kid, and we can't do that alone! This journey has made me less judgmental and more eyes up for other moms and dads in need. I know that a teacher will help me out when I'm not on top of my game, a friend will rescue me at a moment's notice, and I will look to do the same for other busy parents in the trenches when I get the opportunity.

Some of our most healing moments have come from serving others. I decided in the first summer after the loss that we needed to honor Shane's birthday in a special way instead of dreading its approach. I let the boys decide what we were doing. His birthday is the 26th, and so they wanted to make 26 sack lunches for the people experiencing homelessness in downtown Tulsa and deliver them. You see, Shane used to sing at the chapel service at John 3:16 Mission. Our oldest was just a baby, and we would sit and listen, then visit with the families while they had dinner. Shane used to randomly give money to strangers because he felt led to do so. He purchased numerous soccer jerseys

for other kiddos, paid for coaches' hotel stays, and gave willingly to so
many. I was raised with almost zero extra money and learned so much
from him about giving. Since that first birthday, we have done so many
fun and meaningful things in his honor. My favorite was helping the
boys tie scarves to the stop signs downtown in the winter and driving
around later to find some of our homeless friends wearing them.

Luke 6:38 Give, and it will come back to you.

There are so many suggested ways to cope, but they are not the answer
for everyone, and there is no cure for the motion sickness that grief
causes. There is so much research out there about the waves that you
will ride. I want to take some dramamine just thinking about it. The
sleeplessness, fatigue that follows, and initial shock to your body will
indeed improve. Someday. There may not be a timeline. But someday.
I lost about half of my hair within 6 months, and I know looking back
that it was stress and poor nutrition. My oldest son would run for
relief. He had too many miles at the beginning, but he now manages
it, along with a good protein intake, to achieve balance. My precious,
gentle giant middle child would need to occasionally yell into his
pillow. He once broke every trophy in his room. He told me that they
didn't matter anymore because he won them with Dad's help. He and
I glued them all back together, and they are now a reminder of how we
will all put our lives back together despite our emotional brokenness.
My littlest has definite moments of realization about the absence of his
father. You can certainly not underestimate the power of developmen-
tal thinking. A child's brain can only handle so much at a time, and
like with learning to walk, talk, or read, they will develop according to
what their minds can handle at each stage. Being patient with each of
them has been essential. They are so patient with me. We forgive each
other for our bad days, and we have come to realize that we are four
individuals all dealing with the same sadness in our own way.

Isaiah 40:29 He gives strength to the weary…

I could write all day about examples of our daily life and how much we wish he were still here to help us find our way. The hard fact is that he isn't. I recently found a letter that I wrote him just one year after his passing. There is only one good way to take a successful trip, and that is with a compass that never breaks.

'I love you so much that it physically hurts. I know it is time for me to get strong again. To realize that you have equipped these boys with a love of the Lord who is the only real source of strength. How many times did you marvel at their prayers? I still do and am so grateful that the foundation was laid by your example of faith.'

Each of the boys has a specific verse that they feel fits their needs, and we all agree that that Psalms 91:4 fits our whole family, offering us confidence in knowing we are protected while we continue this journey. Our journey has been imperfect, but is made manageable by faith, family, and love.

# A Collection of Haikus

## New Outlook

Sunrises are blank
Sunsets are now vanilla
Come back to us, please.

## Music Heals

Some songs are just yours
Your beautiful soul is free
Like red birds in flight

## Get to Work

Can you help from there?
Throw us the Hail Mary now
We will win for you.

## Bond that Binds

Your friends miss you, too
Glue to our broken, sad hearts
Scattered, yet present

SAY HIS NAME! TELL ME MORE!!

# Say Yes to Yearning. . .
# A Widow's Guide to Valentine's

2/13/19

A few weeks ago, my friend sent me these texts:

**LINDSEY**

I had the most vivid dream last night that I came over and Shane was back. We hugged so tight and told each other how much we missed each other. We all had family dinner and laughed and talked. It was the GREATEST. Just wanted you to know he came to say hi and all is good. 💜 💜 love you.

My broken heart will make it another day! Thank you so much for sharing this. We had lunch with Chris and Mandi yesterday in Norman after the boys games and I was losing it on the way home with a car full of sleeping people. Chris makes me miss him so much more. We talked about work, etc. It's been a hard few weeks. This makes it all better! ♥

I'm sorry it's been tougher than normal. Sometimes I think when someone is hurting a little extra it can block out things while you sleep. So maybe he came to say hi through me to make sure you know. Jen it was the greatest feeling.

**LINDSEY**

I walked in and saw him and squealed "YOU'RE BACK!" He laughed so big. We actually talked a ton about Tate. It was just really peaceful. You were in the kitchen making dinner and would pop in the convo. It was so vivid.

Thank you ♥ ♥ ♥ ♥
I will expect a visit soon!!!!!

Yes! I bet those are the best night. Love you and if you need me. Call me. 💜

So, yes, I have the greatest friends in the world. They know me. They know that while this could be potentially upsetting, it is what I want to hear. Say his name! Tell me more!! Every time I am around certain men with whom he spent a lot of time, glimpses of him are so evident. Mannerisms that friends share and jokes that originated when he was here. A Shane sighting! Have I seen him in my dreams? Yes, many times. Have I seen him lately? Sadly, no.

There is a family of cardinals that lives behind my school. Last year, on the day my school celebrated my Teacher of the Year breakfast, they were playing in the grass in a big group. I hadn't seen them for probably a month before that very morning. I told my friends that I really only think Shane had two regrets in our married years. First, not dancing with me at my sister's wedding (there just wasn't time) and missing my teacher of the year celebration when I taught elementary (he had a meeting at work). He didn't miss this last one. The trees where the cardinals lived were trimmed this fall by the power company. I haven't seen them since.

To say that I have learned the true meaning of the word 'yearn' is an understatement. An extreme longing for something or someone lost. People yearn for the remote when it's missing, a favorite shoe that's gone AWOL as you need to walk out the door, that one shin guard, baseball glove, the nail clippers, a sock...but a person? A huge personality like Shane's leaves a void that not many people can fill. But is he lost like a sock? No. He is very much whole, healed, and living beyond his best life. Billy Graham described heaven as the perfection we long for and that all of the things that made Earth tragic will be gone. These words give me hope.

This week brings Valentine's Day, and our church started a 4-part message series yesterday on Relationship Goals. What is in that for a widow? My oldest son was up and ready for the 8:30 am service. I told him that

I had considered watching from home today due to the content. He was ok with that but I felt like a jerk! He is in his dating years! I need to get over my cheap self. We went, and I prayed that I would see it through his eyes. I prayed that there would be something in that sensitive content that would not amplify my current yearning but aid in the foundation upon which my sons' future love should be built.

The Lord delivered big time! Shane and I had it. We weren't perfect. We fussed over laundry, bills, and discipline for our boys. We loved big right back. We enjoyed each other and made a great pair. We had lofty goals that probably haunt me the most. Giant retirement plans that included hitting up every bluegrass festival from coast to coast in our dreamy RV. We were going to stop along the way to visit the kids, bringing the grandkids back home with us, only to ship them back to their parents in due time. My fellow widow friend and I often discuss how sweet, older couples create the most triggers for us. Yesterday's message was full of reminders. I sat and cried through the end of it, not because I was upset, but because I was so darn proud of what we had.

So, if you are fortunate to have your special someone near you, pray with them. Find that spiritual intimacy for Valentine's Day. I may light a candle and pray with Shane. The yearning will never end, but sometimes it is way worse than others. Shane will 'show up' for me when God knows I need him most. Show up for each other, both in ways that are expected and in ways that are least expected. All of you beautiful singles, pray for what's next. I grew up a child of divorce, and that is a very special kind of grieving. Get your friends together for a Gal-entine's Day lunch and know you are here for a very special reason!! The important thing for us to remember is that even in the never-ending winters of our lives, when it seems like the warmth of the sun will never grace our skin again, Jesus is there cheering us on, and all we have to do is know where to lean.

MY DAYS OF JUDGING ANYONE FOR HOW THEY HANDLE GRIEVING ARE LONG GONE.

# The Holy Spirit and Merle

5/2/19

As widows, we have so many things we might long for, but there are times when I literally BEG God to show me Shane. A breeze with his soapy smell wrapped inside of it, the subtle song of a wind chime, a cardinal in an unexpected place. It's not that I don't trust that he's basking in Heavenly glory; I know he's there and enjoying a front-row seat to all that the boys and I are doing. I just need him near me from time to time. It doesn't always come in my timing, but when it happens…it is perfection.

My days of judging anyone for how they handle grieving are long gone. Shane and I attended two funerals the year before he passed, and they were both very different. He had sung at so many services over the years and was used to standing on stage with the coffin or over the coffin in front of him. He had been hidden off to the side once. We had seen a coffin signed with Sharpies and at another service, just a large, gorgeous photo of our friend. We had some interestingly prophetic dinner conversation following those services. I will be forever grateful for these insights.

It's what comes after the final arrangements that I struggle with at times. From standing in our front yard and screaming at him early on, to discussing life with his ashes that I have saved for my boys. Sometimes you just need to visit. I want to see more of him, and on weeks like this last one, when we were leading up to the anniversary of losing him. I want to will him into existence. My prayers were not yet answered, and I was having a weary day of my usual favorite things. Teach school, pick up my youngest, go to the gym with the boys, run home to change, and head to a football meeting, followed by my niece's softball game. The changing of the clothes part is routine, and I was going for comfort and warmth for a chilly evening game.

We were headed home from the game when I got a lengthy text from an unknown number and decided to read it the second I pulled in my driveway:

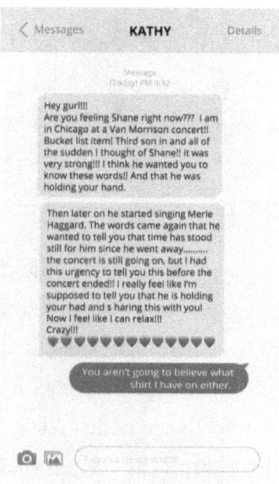

I was taken aback. I told this mystery number two things…one, that the number wasn't programmed into my phone, and two…

Ummmm, wow! That quick change that happened after gym and before the meeting turned out to play a significant role in my evening. I had not worn that shirt before that night in maybe almost a year. The mystery messenger turned out to be a friend that I used to teach with and have known for years. She went on to remind me that she never met Shane. In all of our years of knowing one another, she never had. She listed specific lyrics that he wanted me to hear…'Time has stood still since we've been apart' and 'I can't stop loving you'. She felt such an overwhelming urgency and acted on it. I am so thankful that she did. I just cried and celebrated all evening. My boys were excited for me, and I couldn't wait to share this story.

'Big City', 'Working Man Blues', 'I Think I'll Just Stay Here', 'Ramblin' Fever'…the list goes on and on. These are all songs that my amazingly talented husband, Shane, used to feature when he played at local BBQ joints, wedding receptions, or in a friend's backyard around the fire pit. He loved Merle and all of the old country artists. They were geniuses on guitar, had the best bands around, and spoke the nasty truth on their feelings about life. I miss that. Shane was a truth teller, too. He was once asked to join a church staff after filling in for a few months when they were without a music pastor and refused, saying, 'I don't trust my witness on that stage. I love Jesus, but I like to drink a beer now and then and don't always say the right thing.' Did he still have a gift that only comes from up above? Absolutely.

Did my friend, Kathy, know that I had been up at night pleading with God for a glimpse of my lost love? No. God knew! Many examples of this have occurred in our lives since losing Shane. I like to recognize and share them because I am always so encouraged to know that we are covered and loved on by the Holy Spirit. Many might explain things away as a coincidence, but there is proof in these verses.

John 3:8 (NIV) The wind blows wherever it pleases. You hear its sound, but you cannot tell where it comes from or where it is going. So it is with everyone born of the Spirit. Psalm 105:4 (MSG) Keep your eyes open for God, watch for his works; be alert for signs of his presence.

And the verse that has lifted my spirits and kept me sane over and over again since we joined this club we didn't ask to be a part of: Psalms 91:4 He will cover you with his feathers, and under his wings you will find refuge.

I am grateful for so much despite our circumstances. I am thankful to share my feelings on the subject of loss in hopes that it will help someone else who is hurting. I am blessed by the tribe of friends who surround me. They encircle the boys and me when we desperately need it. I am most grateful for the promptings of the Holy Spirit, who uses us as a vessel to pour out His love cn others.

Kathy sent me a message the next day. We were both trying to unpack all that had happened at her bucket list concert. She and her husband had enjoyed the concert with another couple. Both of the women wanted to gift me their concert t-shirts, feeling like I had been there with them, enjoying it with my man. I was there. He was, too. And Merle has been on repeat ever since.

YOU LOSE INVITATIONS TO NORMAL
THINGS BECAUSE PEOPLE ARE AFRAID
TO INVITE YOU WITHOUT HIM.

# YOLO

5/15/19

When you are going through loss, it holds true that you don't just lose your spouse or loved one but you lose your norm. You lose invitations to everyday things because people are afraid to invite you without him. You lose your sense of importance to other couples you used to hang out with frequently. No doubt about it, no matter how many kiddos you have…it can feel lonely.

My husband's friend was shy. He was in his mid-twenties and hadn't dated much at all. Before having kids, he and Shane could pick guitars until 3 am and never play the same song twice. When they performed in public, people often thought they were brothers. He was pretty much part of our family and we always hoped he would find the perfect match. One night, a beautiful girl came to listen to them play with some of her friends, and they made a connection.

He was so shy and hesitant to engage in the simplest of conversations with this new love interest. We were trying our best to coach him along. Shane even drove him 2 hours one time and hid around the corner while he delivered a gift to her porch. Sending flowers would have been too easy and just not meant as much. It was a blossoming romance.

We accompanied them on a double date for their first outing. Our friend felt better about this and we had a ball! Live music at a historic venue?? Don't mind if we do! It was the perfect evening. We spent a lot of time together after this night and their love and our friendships grew strong. We were in their wedding. It was gorgeous and their families welded together fairly seamlessly.

Fast forward to about a year after we lost Shane. The boys and I had visited them several times while passing through their town for sports. We stayed with them once, and he played guitar with my middle boy, who started lessons after Shane's passing. His wife and I just watched in wonder, both of us tearing up at the beauty of the music and what a testament it was to the friendship that has built all of this. The whole scene was a picture of grieving and coping, of love and support in our darkest times.

About 6 months after our stay, she called. She was leaving him, and she thought I might understand since life is short. Y'all, I didn't hear much else. I'm sorry, but those statements seem to be reserved for things like skydiving, swimming with sharks, eating the world's hottest pepper?? Certainly not for breaking a covenant made with forever in mind.

Living on the edge can be fun, but how does one make a comparison like this? I am a child of divorce and so was Shane. We were determined never to parent solo, and here I am. While I will never know every reason why that happened, I was hurt by the delivery and now grieving a marriage that I just knew was forever.

I was recently sitting at a dinner party with friends. A rare event for me, as I have three athletes to tend to. It was nice until someone started joking around, and I made a reference to something Shane would have said. It stopped one friend in her tracks. Maybe we aren't around each other often enough for her to know that I find it perfectly acceptable to talk about him like he is still right here. Maybe it's because she didn't know him like some of the others there, but it made her uncomfortable enough to sigh and leave shortly after. That's ok.

I try not to take too many things personally. I genuinely don't feel lonely when my boys are gone for an evening, or I am driving somewhere without them. I feel the loneliest in instances like this. An outcast in a way. Now used as a mile marker for validation of someone's horrible decision and a reason for someone to skulk out of a party early. I am learning to love my life but I may never love it all.

I had the amazing privilege of hearing Bob Goff speak last week. I immediately started reading his book, 'Love Does'. He tells a quite hilarious story about his wedding cake and how he watched it fall to the asphalt in the parking lot on the way to the reception. He and the baker scooped it back up and made a plan. The baker went on an icing run, gathered the larger pieces of cake, and served it up. He talks about how God uses broken people. Shattered people, even, not just as bystanders but participants.

I can still make a difference to others around me. I can still be a part of a conversation, a solution to a friend's problem, a listening ear, or a mentor to a student who has lost someone special to them. I can be myself. I don't have to hide my love for Shane even though it's been

4 years since he's been gone. I don't have to NOT have an opinion or play a valuable role in my children's foundation.

I firmly believe what Bob says about broken people, "…my life is full of rocks, pieces of asphalt, broken and unrepaired relationships, and unwanted debris. But somehow God allows us to be served up anyway." Mr. Goff goes on to discuss the diverse range of people Jesus would serve, from loose women to lawyers like him. "The only thing Jesus said He couldn't serve up were people who were full of themselves or believed the lie that they were who they used to be before they met Him."

I am who God has made me to be. I will do my best to live unapologetically the path that He set before me. Gravel and all! Serve me up, Lord. Don't allow others to use my story as their excuses, but please allow me to blaze a trail for others to appreciate everything God has given them and not take life for granted.

I OFTEN TELL PEOPLE
THAT WE DON'T IDLE WELL.

# Ease In

5/30/19

I am a teacher, and while I used to look forward to a good break from school, all of that changed when I lost Shane, not just for me, but for my boys as well. It's as if we've lost the ability to know how to rest and reset. I often tell people that we don't idle well.

I couldn't close my eyes at first. Not even to sleep at night. I lost about ½ of my head of hair in the first year due to stress and lack of sleep. Fortunately, I have a lot to spare, but I would gauge it on how many times my ponytail holder could wrap around it. It went from barely 2 to easily 4. I still struggle with sleep. Nothing was easy anymore. The summer immediately following his death, my boys and I sat outside my sister's house in the car and prayed we could make it through a routine yearly pool party with my school family. I can remember our first winter break without him. He worked regular hours, so it's not like he was home during these breaks, but he used to take one day off on winter break. I intentionally MADE us leave the house at least once a day that year. We would mostly go shoot baskets at the YMCA. We weren't ready for the movies, or bowling…certainly not mentally prepared to rush out of town unless it was for a game. There was just no peace in our rest, and being around too many others was not enjoyable for anyone involved.

Over the past few years, we have been working on this. My boys are right back to groveling over closet cleanouts and lawn mowing rotations when summer hits because they have better things to do. I am so happy for us! There should be no immediate shame in smiling, in laughing at a joke, or in planning a trip. The reality of your lost loved one missing out is a real struggle. You feel like you shouldn't be doing any living without them here, as if it isn't respectful to them.

My youngest is now 11, and this week, he has been so kind to accompany me to water aerobics. We haven't missed a day yet and we are quite enjoying ourselves. I was in a walking boot for 5 months last year. My Achilles doesn't want to cooperate with the rest of my leg. To avoid surgery since not working or not driving isn't an option for me, I was in 11 weeks of physical therapy. My physical therapist told me to get in the water, and he was right! The pool is my friend. I knew that once school was out, I wanted to make this a habit, but I didn't realize how much it would bless my soul!

If you haven't seen the new movie 'Poms', you must go. Get a group of friends, or go alone (I like doing this and did not think I would). It is a heartwarming tale of senior sisterhood, set in a retirement community called Sun Springs. Well, on our first day at water aerobics, my son whispered and asked if we were at Sun Springs. I am 44, and a young member of this class, while he's 11, and he doesn't realize it, but he's the star of the show. How sweet it is to get advice on movements from these seasoned pros? How lovely it is to see the friendships and the life lessons they are sharing? I don't even like to be seen in a swimsuit. I teach 7th graders and always know someone wherever we go. I just know I will end up on someone's snapchat story or instagram in all my glory. Well, here, it doesn't matter. This class is about being STRONG, NOT SKINNY! My friend told me once that that was her goal. I like it! I love the strong part in every sense of the word. At my local YMCA's version of Sun Springs, they are all there for the benefits of joint health, cardio, and companionship. It is just what the doctor ordered!

The other fantastic thing about this class is that I recognized the instructor. She is a greeter at our church. It is a large church, with multiple services, and I had never visited with her until now. She is noticeably shy, and I was surprised to see her as the instructor. Another sweet lady in class asked how the boys and I were doing and made a reference to Shane. The instructor was standing close by and told me that she, too, had lost her husband. She went on to say that she had a horrible breakdown after all of her children were grown and gone. She had held it together until then. She had raised them to their fullest, most productive adult selves. Her mom job was done, and she didn't know what to do next. She was so wonderful to tell me this. She encouraged me to address the difficult things now. Again, the people that are in our path are God-breathed.

So, here is my go at easing into a break and living life with no guilt, not bottling up sadness, and showing my boys vulnerability. It is a burdensome concept to grasp and even more grueling to accept without Shane. I replied to someone who was hurting recently with this list of things to do when I can't sleep. Perhaps this can be of help to someone and offer assistance to you or someone you know.

**Can't rest:**

1.  Get up! Don't sit or lie there and think about how much you can't sleep. I will walk my neighborhood street at 3 am if needed. I keep my garage open in case one of the boys wakes up and I don't go far...just back and forth in the fresh air. I often pray walk, meaning that I pray aloud while taking a stroll. So far, no HOA complaints, and I find this so fulfilling. Usually, I am more at peace when I am finished. I sometimes make my way upstairs to pray over my boys while they sleep.

2.  Do something you hate. Laundry – It is one of my least favorite chores. When I can't rest, it's always there. With three stinky boys in sports, I can always start a load, finish my hang ups, or pair those dang socks. You will be happy that you knocked something off your daily chores and not as frazzled from lack of sleep. Productive in a sense. 'The secret to getting ahead is getting started.' -Mark Twain

3.  Read!! I recently got a new bookshelf for all of my books. I don't like reading on my phone because I rely on it so much for the boys' schedules and teams, so I don't enjoy staring at it to read. I prefer paperbacks and love having them on hand to share with my friends. One of the best things I have done in the last year was joining a book club. It is one of my two scheduled outings a month: book club and Bunco. What can I say, I'm a wild woman!

4.  Clean out a drawer. Pathetic, you would think I would be embarrassed to even type that. But who doesn't have a junk drawer?

5.  Listen to a Podcast. Listening can be done while doing almost any of the above. 'A Frayed Knot' is one of my favorites. Fresh Life Church with Levi Lusko. Anything Craig Groeschel.

6.  Journaling. I have a prayer journal, and when a prayer is answered, I mark it down. The dates are always interesting and often so telling. God's timing is by no means our own, and I love to see how He works.

7.    Active meditation. You can find these guided meditations on Apple music, YouTube, or your favorite streaming service. Some are designed to help you scan your body for tension, while others are better suited for self-talk and calming your mind.

8.    Gardening. While this is hard to do at 3 am, I have been known to pull weeds at all hours. I love my garden. Something about new life and dirt lights my fire. I love sharing the salsa I make each summer. I don't eat anything spicy, but I can grow a mean jalapeño.

At the height of my anxiety, I have tried any and all of these things. I know there are many more that would help. I also could have listed things like: look through old photos, smell that one shirt I still thinks smells just like him, listen to the songs I have that he recorded, stare at my wedding dress, take out the notes I found while cleaning out his office at work (some of them are drawings of football plays for Lane's team) or just sit and feel sorry for myself. These options are not healthy for me every time. I still resort to them and use them when I think I can handle it. I am grateful to be somewhat over a black diamond mogul of grief and able to relax a little on breaks. My to-do list is always long, and my sights are maybe too high on what all I can get accomplished before the hustle and bustle starts all over again. I know Shane would be proud of how far we have come. May you find some guilt-free peace today!

THEY HAD A GREAT EXAMPLE TO FOLLOW,
EVEN IF JUST FOR A LITTLE WHILE.

# You Already Have. . .
## Coping on Father's Day

6/14/19

Father's Day is hard. The End.

That statement could literally be this whole post and would probably ring true to many of you. My dad didn't live with us after I turned 9. He had, and still has, another life. One where the four of us original kids of his are in a different state, and while that's a whole other story, there's love there, and a lot of healing has managed to take place over the years. As a widow with children, my concern on Father's day is for them. It's just a tricky Sunday that requires some processing.

As the day approaches, I am trying something new this year. I will be presenting each of my boys with a letter about how they remind me of their dad. Part of doing this has been to seek out someone they might be able to relate to who has lost someone special. There are many people in our lives who have, and some I don't believe my boys are aware of. I think this will be a nice way for them to remember they are not alone. My husband was a musician, and who doesn't love Keith Urban? In doing a little research for my Father's Day idea, I realized that he wrote a song and released it in 2002 called 'Song for Dad'. He then lost his dad to cancer in 2015. The same year we lost Shane. There is a beautiful photo of him and his dad online. There is the most beautiful line in this song that I want my boys to own this next year, it mentions that when someone says they hope they get to meet your dad, you just need to smile and say that they already have.

Tate, Your careful thoughts about the world. Your honest skepticism about certain ideas. Your gentle way with your little brothers. Your drive. Your bravery.

Lane, Your tenderness and compassion. Your manly charm and quiet way of helping others without expecting anything in return. Your strength. Your heart.

Wyatt, Your smart mouth and sass. Your build and your perfect hairline. Your determination. Your ability to go against the flow with grace. Your spirit.

These are just a few ways that I was able to express to them that they are his boys through and through. They all have his eyes. That's easy, but to really dig in and pinpoint what I see in them that is a direct reflection of Shane was emotional and therapeutic all at the same time. I wish he were just here. I would love for him to be at Wyatt's game Sunday, cheering him on, coaching him up, and enjoying a victory dinner with us after the final whistle. It's ok to wish.

I never want my boys to forget that celebrating a Father who loved them unconditionally makes it a good day, even when he's not here.

Someday, they will be the ones being celebrated. They had a great example to follow, even if just for a little while. Their dad would be so proud of them.

May you all find a way to honor the dads in your life. May my children be blessed and know that their mother is doing her very best to show enough love for both. And while I know everyone's story is different, may we take comfort in a safe community to share our struggles and to be lifted up.

I HAVE BEEN WORKING ON A
STAND-UP ROUTINE IN MY HEAD
FOR AT LEAST A DECADE.

# SNL Wanna Be

6/28/19

"Women are nearly twice as likely as men to be diagnosed with an anxiety disorder in their lifetime." –ADAA, Anxiety and Depression Association of America. I found this website to be particularly helpful in many ways. They have a variety of articles and first hand stories through blog posts from PTSD survivors, helping introverts, and how to handle numerous types of anxiety. My favorites are humor-based solutions.

Oftentimes, we are too serious. It is the worst when you feel like you can't find humor in anything anymore. I have been there so many times. My boys are a constant source of entertainment. They are fluent in sarcasm. I guess not all mothers would consider this a character trait to be proud of for their children, but they are also extremely well-mannered, so I will take the balance.

I have been working on a stand-up routine in my head for at least a decade. Coming from a family like mine, you have to just roll with the humor and not take things too seriously. My sisters and I often ask why we don't have our own show. We don't, and no network would probably hire us, but if it brightens someone's day, then it's a win for me. Some of these bits come from personal experience...ok, all of them do. So, here goes nothing.

**You know you're raising boys if:

- You have to ask if they remembered to wear undies, and you keep an extra pair in the glove box.

- You can't quite put your finger on the stench in your car and then realize there were a pair of football shoulder pads left in the very back overnight.

- You reach under the seat while cleaning trash out of the car and accidentally grab a protective cup.

- You praise them when they actually reach the trash can with any and all items.

- The word balls cannot possibly be uttered without a laugh and you literally search your brain for any and all other ways to word something without saying BALLS (this also pertains to my job of teaching 7th graders).

**At a family reunion and my oldest saw a boombox with a stack of CD's next to it. He asked me if that was an 8 track player??!!!

**We always say that our family tree is best described as a flow chart.

\*\*My oldest has been on a t-ball team with his uncle as a teammate. Yes, my brother-in-law is my son's age and we love him! Let's embrace it all!

\*\*My sweet niece, who lives in a large city near us and has a magnificent pool in her backyard, once asked if our pond was heated. Ummmm, no sugar.

\*\*Kids are always using the wrong words in the cutest ways. Teaching 7th grade science, without fail, a student will use the word 'orgasm' for 'organism'. Try not to laugh or even crack a smile when that happens, and part of the class is wide-eyed, awaiting your reaction.

I remember as a kid at church camp hearing someone tell us that if we were worried about something out of our control, we should write it down and then tear it into a million pieces and throw it away. Remember, I was a kid, so they didn't likely say ONE MILLION pieces but work with me here. I am going to write out some irrational mom fears that seem ridiculous once they are out of my mind. I am going to guess that many of you might be caught shaking your head, yes, at the screen. I've got ONE MILLION more, but here are a couple that come right to mind.

\*\*Why do large discount stores put cement structures in front of their doors leading to the parking lot? My logical guess is that they think a rogue car coming at the entrance will hit those first? My mom brain tells me it is to drive me crazy. Since conception, my boys have been plotting ways to launch themselves over them and into the building. When mine were younger, I could envision the top of the red target cement ball like a mini trampoline launching them back into oncoming traffic.

\*\*Ever forgotten the bug spray or sunscreen? I immediately think that mine are getting the West Nile virus if they seem overly tired on the drive home from the 4th of July BBQ. Ummm, no crazy lady, they have been running wild for the last 6 hours. Swimming in an overcrowded pool, eating preservative infested junk, dodging smoke bombs, taking mental notes on how to light a fire, inhaling toxic fumes, probably have a 2nd degree sunburn, possible botulism from under-cooked hot dogs over the fire, and let's not forget they might already be developing a staph infection from an untreated stubbed toe while playing tag in the dark. All three of mine didn't just lose their first teeth in a sweet wiggly moment; all three of them had that tooth knocked out in various ways, so I have a right to be concerned.

In all seriousness, I developed an anxiety disorder about a year before my husband passed. It was a hard time in my life. Everything at home was in near perfect order, but I was beyond worried for a friend that was dying right before my eyes. There was nothing I could do to help her, and it was bringing up all sorts of emotions that are out of my control. I have discovered that I like to be in control. One example is that I prefer to drive if going somewhere in a group. I feel out of control when I am a passenger. I don't consider myself a dramatic person and would never throw a fit to be the driver. I will sit quietly and mull over all of the things that could possibly go wrong. I guess behind the wheel, my mind is busy. Too busy to think of the things that could go wrong at my own expense.

I will be fast asleep and wake up with a jolt, run to the door of my room before I ever realize I have left my cozy bed. I will sit in church if it is too hot or too cold and genuinely believe that I can't get out of the room. I will hide in the storage room between classes at school, just catching my breath. It is a real and horrible feeling. Real. Anxiety is real. Acknowledge it and find help and ways to cope.

These are things I have discovered by being honest with myself. Anxiety is terrifying. People joke all the time, "I nearly had a panic attack!!" Well, I pray you never experience a real one. The science behind it is fascinating, but I don't wish it on my worst enemy…not even the mom who was yelling my kid's jersey number at a game once because she was wanting someone to 'take him out' since he was clearly doing his job by dominating her child…and I wished a lot of things on her. Even nudged my neighbor and gave her the go ahead to say something if needed. We've got to have each other's backs, but a panic attack? No, I don't even wish that on her.

I WANT TO TELL THEM TO NOT CHEAPEN
THE EXPERIENCE FOR THEIR CHILD.

# Loving Enough for Two

7/15/19

The mind of a solo parent is like a one-legged duck trying to swim. I am in constant turmoil about what the right thing to say or do might be, and my biggest concern is trying so hard to shower them with enough love, acceptance, and encouragement from both their dad and me.

We are a sports family. We live and breathe whichever sport is in season and usually more than one sport at a time. I have 3 athletes. I am not bragging, but I will tell you that as a sports mom, there is a difference between a kid who just wants the camaraderie of a team and a kid who is out there to develop as an athlete. I have three athletes. Is it healthy at their ages to say they always want the win? To say that they watch video after video to improve a move, a lift, a tackle, a skill? To say that they want to miss fun outings to go to extra training? I have always believed that it is what has kept my sons grounded and engaged.

I was a very small part of the Twisters Soccer Dynasty of Owasso, OK. We were good before there was club ball…before there was multi-level competition. My parents divorced shortly after we had won our first state title. My husband used to tease me that we were the only 3rd grade team in the state at that time. He could tease because while I was backing off of team sports to help my mom out, he was trudging forward in every sport available. We decided that the only sport he wasn't good at was soccer because he never played it…until we joined an adult co-ed league. My husband grew up in Texas, where football was serious business, and his family chose Owasso when they moved during his Senior year, all because of the baseball program. My boys happen to be surrounded by men who were college athletes. A goal they currently hope to achieve.

Now comes the hard part for a mom. I'm not a man. I don't know the ins and outs of the locker room. I don't know when it is appropriate for me to step in and ask a coach advice for applications, exactly how much money should be spent on ID camps and recruiters, and whether or not a good Division 1 school with a little offer vs. a good NAIA school with a better offer will translate well when they apply for their first real job. I'm not in the coach's ear like some dads, and I don't have time to volunteer like some moms, unless it's behind the scenes. There are politics in sports, but my kids know that their dedication and hard work are what will earn them a spot on the team. Nothing else.

I don't always have the right advice for my boys when they feel down about their performance. My husband was also a musician but didn't learn to play the guitar until he was a teenager. I know this could apply to any child's interests. They are extremely hard on themselves in all aspects of life, and those are the moments that no matter what I say, it wouldn't matter. Dr. Jill Bolte discusses a 90-second rule for emotional response. I have been trying to use this time with my boys.

My initial thoughts are usually the exact opposite of how they feel about a situation, so if I just sit with them in the moment and let them unpack their thoughts, they tend to become more rational as time passes. If I'm being honest, this is completely unnatural and difficult, yet incredibly beneficial.

When we lost Shane, he had coached every one of the boys' sports except our youngest. He had only had the pleasure of watching him play his first few little bunch ball YMCA basketball seasons and he had watched him break his first boards at his Little Dragons karate class. My boys have never lost the desire to be involved in a team. Our sports families bless us and while it is a lot of work for everyone, I have found that we are indeed a family. I know that someday, when my boys have their own children, they will have plenty of funny travel stories to tell and life lessons to share, no matter what their kids want to be involved in. My oldest sister and her husband have traveled the states with my boys, helping me support them. My boys have traveled alone with their teams when needed. This was a huge anxiety trigger for me, but I know how much they learned in branching out.

So, why am I rambling about this? I want you to know you are not alone if you are a widow raising men. There are people out there who will have a heart for your kids. Pray for them. Pray for the men who cross their paths and the influence that they will have on them. Pray for open communication between your budding athlete and yourself. That your kids will tell you when they need you, and that you have the willpower to keep your distance and let them soar. Taking a backseat is the hardest part for me. I want to fix everything for them. I want to tell the parents who don't see their kids doing great things to take note of every encouragement they offer a teammate after a tough loss, every team prayer they voluntarily lead, every borrowed sock or shin guard, and every handshake. I want to tell the tryhard parents that their child will make a name for themselves if you trust the process and let them. I want to ask them not to cheapen the experience for their child.

The hardest part for me as a mom has been to TRUST those around me. Not everyone is out for your child's best interest if it hinders their agenda, but I have to trust that God's plan is bigger than any agenda. The verse he laid on my heart after losing Shane will continue to hold true even when my heart is giving all it can, and it doesn't always feel like enough. Psalm 91:4

IF I AM DOING IT WRONG,
I ONLY HAVE MYSELF TO BLAME,
SO NO NEED TO HELP ME OUT WITH THAT.

# Can We Please Stop:

7/31/19

- Dreading going places where people might feel sorry for us?
  Girl, sit alone if you want and read your book. Go to a movie by
  yourself or have dinner. Go to the party where you know it will
  be mostly couples... you got the invite, so just go and be with
  your friends! Attend all the weddings and let them remind you
  to celebrate true love with a box of tissues if needed!

- Questioning what is the right thing to do for us, or how it
  will appear to others? Wear your ring or don't wear your ring.
  I personally still wear my band. My sister and I often take my
  boys places together, and people assume we are a couple. It
  has happened so many times that my boys now point it out.
  We embrace it and let them keep thinking what they want. I
  have quit caring so much about what others think of me. My
  beautiful engagement ring made me so sad every time it would

sparkle while I was making a turn with the steering wheel. I have to drive… a lot, actually. I will never forget how nervous he was when he gave me that ring, and maybe one of my boys will feel that same feeling one day and want to use it. He had a perfectly planned evening and took me to dinner at a place where we would end up taking the boys to vacation every summer. Then, we decided that we would take his ashes there, as it would be the best place for us to visit. All of the greatest things started with that ring.

- Thinking we aren't enough for our children? Y'all, the judgment that can come from other parents is real. I'm acutely aware that you may have handled something differently than I did with my boys, but there is a lot of prayer and petition that goes into every decision I make for them and with them. If I am doing it wrong, I only have myself to blame, so there's no need to help me out with that. Find yourself a sound support system that won't judge you for your parenting, but will be there for you WHEN you ask them. Parenting is very personal. While it does take a village, I choose to keep my village very small when it comes to direct advice and interaction. I have one of the very best around!

- Wishing away the days ahead because of the days we thought they would be? I have written so much about this very thing. I wanted more! I still do, and I have decided that it's okay to yearn for what is no longer. That pain is so very real, and loving some-one that much really does prove that the memories are alive even though Shane is not. It just tears me up to admit that. Four years out, and I am still tempted to call or text him first when something amazing happens. I keep writing blessings down so that if my boys ever doubt how far we have come, all I have to do is show them.

- Limiting our ceiling? We all have a lot of life left to live, even if just a day. Don't second-guess things you want to try or goals you wish to accomplish. Don't wait. You have it in you! A precious friend in my water aerobics class told me that she knew I would miss this when school started back. She even offered to come and watch a class for me so I could come back to class with the ladies once in a while. I don't know this lady very well AT ALL, but she must see the joy that the class brings to me. I don't really know what possessed me to think that was a good idea this summer, but I have only missed a handful of days. Just step out and try something new...for YOU. Next on my list is Tai Chi. I want to write a book someday. I want to travel, and even though that was OUR dream for when the boys graduated, I plan to make it happen.

When you're feeling low or unsure of your abilities as a mom, your future, your dreams, or even your social calendar, listen to this and remember that there is always hope. Thank you, sweet Savior, for what you say to me. Lauren Daigle reminds us that he says we are loved even when we can't feel it. We are strong when we only feel weak. We are held tight when we feel like we fall short. When we are feeling the pit of loneliness, we belong to the Lord. We are His!

HE HAS BEEN THROUGH TOO MUCH AT HIS AGE, AND HE MANAGES TO RISE ABOVE IT ALL EVERY DAY.

# Quarterbacking

8/15/19

Raising three boys who love sports leaves me no choice but to begin each Fall with a cram-packed schedule of practices, scrimmages, games, and so on. In the midst of the instant chaos, my heart is weary for the man who helped run this season of the year so flawlessly.

School starts here in a week, and I teach. I have tried so hard to keep my time off the same since losing Shane, because that was a real draw to teaching for me. Shane used to take off a day or two on short breaks, and then we would vacation in the summers. I love the momming that can still happen while teaching and how the teachers in our district 'mother' my children when they aren't with me. Will I always be able avoid a second job in the summers? Maybe not, because I have a Senior this year and I'm not sure exactly how affording everything will work, depending on scholarships, etc. A lot of important decisions and moments are coming right up, which has been ironically the perfect timing for our 'Anxious for Nothing' series at church!

It amazes me that Paul wrote this letter while in prison. He is urging others not to be anxious. Philippians 4:6-7 says, Be anxious for nothing, but in everything by prayer and supplication, with thanksgiving, let your requests be made known to God; and the peace of God, which surpasses all understanding, will guard your hearts and minds through Christ Jesus. Another fantastic example is Matthew 6:27, which simply asks if anyone can add a single hour to their life by worrying. Good perspective. It isn't easy to actually manage these expectations, but they are right there for us to follow. What a relief!

Our oldest has only ever played one season of football in 2nd grade. Shane picked up the last team chosen, mostly consisting of late sign-ups and kids who didn't play the previous year. I can remember him being so relieved after one game that he congratulated the parents and players because not a single kid had cried during that game, and we had finally achieved our first, first down! Well, my oldest didn't fall in love with football as his chosen sport like my other two. Soccer ended up being his passion and still is. This year, his Senior year, he has decided to try kicking for the football team. Picture Adam Sandler in Happy Gilmore as a hockey player showing up for golf. Well, this is Tate— a soccer player showing up for football.

I am a firm believer that kids can do anything they put their minds to. Tate has always stayed in his lane for the most part. He has lived and breathed soccer his whole life, and he loves to run. He is the captain of his ECNL team for both club and varsity and we are in a 6A district. He has been called the quarterback of his club soccer team by his coach. He constantly points to where the next play is happening. When he gets anxious or needs some time to unpack his mind, he runs. He was running marathon-level miles in the days immediately after losing Shane. He discovered about two years ago that he was putting a lot of miles on his legs and started kicking the football to blow off steam. He is a good boy. He has been through too much at his age, and he manages to rise above it all every day. He is a leader, plain and simple. I have three very different boys, but I am so blessed to say they are all leaders. I believe that all children are born to lead in their own way.

I teach STEM, and it amazes me to see the dynamics of a group. There is always a quarterback. Someone who calls the plays, directs the team, and sees the whole field. The most significant part about this is that if a leader does things right, they will delegate responsibilities to the team. They don't have to do it all themselves. I had a parent email me one time, concerned that their child was never paired with their 'intellectual equals' and wanted them to be challenged by others at or above their own mindset. I explained that my grouping is entirely random and that the important thing for the student to learn is that, as a leader, there's no need to take over but to learn from others' differences, and that it's not always about academic growth. We aren't all the same, and that is a beautiful thing. We actually wouldn't learn as much if we were. This is the world we live in. We all have strengths.

I have had to listen to my own advice on this subject. Life can become overwhelming. As solo parents, we have to know our limits. We have to find a team and quarterback the heck out of them on behalf of our family. My sister is basically the world's greatest wide receiver. I can throw anything at her and she will catch it every time. I have friends who are like my very own offensive line. They will stop people in their tracks before they would ever let them mess with me. My little sister is like a running back, quick and direct with her help and encouragement. I can think of every position and see the faces of people who are there for my boys and me. It took me a long time to take advantage of the help that surrounds me. I don't want to lose the game, so I don't plan to do it alone anymore.

Find yourself a team, draw up some plays, and start handing out assignments. Be nurtured and inspired by those around you. Work together to build up your little leaders and encourage them to take risks. Tate is taking a risk like he never has, and I am so proud of him for this. He is straying from his norm and being challenged. He has surrounded himself with a group of people who are lifting him up and encouraging his bravery. One of his coaches, whom God put in our lives a few years ago and who also lost his dad too soon, called me the other night and said that seeing Tate in that element, he just had this overwhelming feeling that someone in Heaven was mighty proud. I couldn't agree more, AG!

MY COUNSELOR ONCE TOLD ME THAT
TRYING TO HOLD ONTO
LONG-TERM MEMORIES
CAN MAKE SHORT-TERM MORE DIFFICULT.

# Bricks

## 9/15/19

At the YMCA pool every weekday morning at 5:30 am, you can find four people; the lifeguard, two lap swimmers, and me. You can also find near silence. Aside from the swish of the water and the hum of the pumps, there is the occasional lifeguard who plays music...but not very loud. The first day I tried this time slot, I was amazed at the dedication of these people this early. One, for a job, and the others, for their health or a triathlon they are training for? Who knows. We don't bother each other. It's an understood quiet time.

Fall is such a frenzy. The rush of school starting back and all that it entails. I am so happy to have some quiet. I often use times when I was alone to reflect and remember. Fall is one of my favorite times for memories. It's like the wind shifts a little, a few leaves fall, and my mind is back to a time when Shane coached every night and our boys hung on his every word. All the way back to when he had planned the perfect proposal, and we were just kids ourselves. My counselor once told me that trying to hold onto long term memories can make short term more difficult. I can no longer remember my new student's names as easily. In my defense, I am now teaching semesters, so I will have close to 275-300 students by year-end. I hate it only because I want to know them all, and their stories stick better than their sweet names.

My little sister recently joined me for a few mornings at the pool. I was shocked to hear of her more than slight fear of water. She is a very successful CrossFit owner who helps change people's lives for a living. She's a gorgeous beast and can do anything. We were raised in the same household, but in very different ways. She asked me if I remembered having swimming lessons. I did, she didn't. That's a whole other blog… about doing hard things and how you never know what someone considers a challenge, and another blog about our childhood depravities.

Fully expecting to sing some old songs in my head or play memory recall, I noticed the bricks. I just looked up and there they were. I thought I might use them to count my laps, and instead, I realized I had several people on my heart to pray for. Every day since, I have decided to pray over each brick. There are 29 of them. I am never short of people who God places on my heart.

My secretaries at school, the tech department for our school system, all of the people at the pediatrician's office, coaches who pour over my boys every day, parents with seniors, parents with first time kindergartners, my boys' teachers, my bosses, our campus pastor and his family, my friend who retired, naming family members and something specific about them, my students (even if just by face for now), my husband's dad, the person I noticed crying in their car at a stop light because I've been there. I could do this all day. I will look up and, no joke, someone will come to mind.

On some of my lowest mornings, I have felt the exact opposite of what you might expect. I will look up to find my first brick, not knowing even who or what will pop into my head, and it will be a praise. There is so much to be thankful for in my life the Holy Spirit is reminding me of that when I am feeling sorry for myself. Things have been revealed to me that I had forgotten about. Little things that were done for our family right after losing Shane. You are in such a fog pretty much that whole first year that I am so happy to be recalling some of these blessings now.

I hear people talk about how lonely they feel. I am fortunate that I have only had a few moments when I have felt truly lonely, and it's often in a room full of people. I am happy about these bricks and what they have revealed to me about my prayer life. How rich it can be and how much there is to be thankful for. How so many people have prayed us through our days and I know they will continue to do so. Now, our pool is closing for maintenance and repairs for the next two weeks, so I have decided that I will need to count the cracks in the sidewalk and am already praying for cooler mornings.

I KNOW YOU SEE US.
I KNOW YOU HEAR US.
I KNOW YOU LOVE US.

# What If I Woke Up One Day and You Were Here

9/27/19

I have dreamed about this moment. What Heaven will be like. I picture you around a fire pit with a dozen or so of your closest friends. It is for some reason a very diverse group. A collection, if you will, of the many people and cultures we grew to love together through sports families, church, work, and music. You look amazing! Happily praising...guitar in hand! I am always a bit envious if I'm being honest.

If you were to return to our lives on Earth now, it would be seamless. We would do most everything the same, but you would be here for me. To listen to my school stories and to encourage me on rough days. To take me on dates when the leaves start to fall and remind me in jest not to get too excited about my birthday coming up because I wasn't getting anything. You always overdid it and made sure the boys made a big deal. I know this is where they get their great gift ideas for friends and family.

We would cheer on our kids throughout life. You would do all the math homework, and I would pretend to help with the English, even though we all know you read more and faster than I do, were a great writer, and loved the classics. Your high school teacher wouldn't believe that one. We would grill and enjoy the dogs together, and you would just love this new Walmart grocery pickup because that would mean more time at home. It's the everyday that gets me sometimes.

I need your help. I need to know what to tell these boys in their worst, most self-doubtful hours. I need help that only you can offer. There are so many well-meaning people around us, but none of them could answer these big questions from your boys. I know you see us. I know you hear us. I know you love us. And, I know where to find these answers, but it would just be a lot easier if you were here.

ALL FOR THE PRICE OF LOVE.

# The Power of a Handwritten Note

2/7/20

My middle son had Flu B. In that week, I managed to miss only a half day of school, while he missed five days. He's old enough to rest on his own and I can check on him throughout the day. Plenty of willing family and friends to come to his rescue if needed. Only one me to get up in the middle of the night, so sleep was at a minimum. My neck hurts, my back hurts, and I've done more yoga stretches in the last week than in a year. All for the price of love.

That one half day produced a one page-long letter from the substitute. My class doesn't work logistically well with a substitute because it is a very busy and noisy inquiry-based environment. They are creating, building, and problem-solving. I had scheduled the day with 30 minutes allocated for group meetings and 30 minutes for quiet individual work. Preparing for a substitute is one of my least favorite parts of teaching because I am very nervous that they will never want to come back. There is a shortage of these precious individuals in our area, and the pennies on the dollar we can offer them is not the only reason. Kids can be hard on a sub. Remember that? "At 9:22, everyone get up and go to the pencil sharpener at the same time! It will be hilarious!" That is a direct quote from a note written by Jeremy in my 5th-grade class, who passed it quietly while we all tried to contain our church giggles. It is the same now, only the notes come more quickly on sneaky texts under the desks.

Upon receiving the sub's note, I was both shocked and dumbfounded at my naivety. But in half a day?? Really guys? After dealing with the specific names left and chatting with each class, I realize that it's not the end of the world, but when you're going on a few hours rest, you're already feeling defeated.

That evening, I received a text from my colleague asking if I had gotten a note from a particular student. She sent me a picture of her's and I swooned. All the heart eyes! I told her that I didn't think we were at this stage of appreciation yet. That he must really love her class. I even reminded her that I just switched to a semester format, so I haven't had him long, and we are still getting used to each other. Why would she give me this heads up? Because we teach 7th grade and the art of a handwritten thank-you note is mostly lost, especially on a 12- or 13-year-old. Our reactions are everything to them about most things, so I was happy to know it wouldn't be a hidden camera joke or that I wasn't being punked if he handed me one, too.

The next morning (and keep in mind, he didn't know how badly I needed this, as he wasn't in the half-day that had a substitute) I was handed the sweetest 3x5 notecard I ever did see. Not only was it written carefully in his best penmanship, but it was so specific and sincere. I took attendance and got the class started, and so as not to embarrass him, I waited until the rush of group work began and quietly told him it may just be the nicest thing that has happened to me in a long time. His response made me even happier.

He said, "Remember the first day of class when you told us that school is the only place that you looked forward to when you were our age? Well, my house can get a bit chaotic, and I decided to thank the people who are there. I got kind of sad and this made me happy."

Write someone a note today. Like now. Just stop and do it. Even if it's short. Even if you have to go get stamps and mail it. Have fun with it. Decorate with stickers or markers or paint. Just write it. There are many people who would love an old fashioned Valentine this time of year. Some of my favorite, but most painful, reminders of Shane are when I unexpectedly find a note he had written me. Priceless. Do it! If you don't have time to write it, text it. Email it. However, writing it will be both fun and fulfilling, and it might even make you happy.

Dear Mrs. Farley,
I just want to thank you for the way you act. You are so calm, especially when helping with the new students. I also want to applaud you for your teaching style. From allowing us to play with cards together, to letting us work with little to no instruction. Your techniques are practical and effective.
Turning my cogwheels

THE FACT THAT OUR HEART YEARNS FOR
SOMETHING EARTH CAN'T SUPPLY IS
PROOF THAT HEAVEN MUST BE OUR HOME.
– C.S. LEWIS

# Sticks, Stones, and Perspective

8/17/20

Last Monday marked our first day back at our physical school building since spring break, and all I could think about was how every other year some of the teachers would meet to walk the building and pray. This is a public school and while I'm sure not every parent would agree that it is necessary, we consider it a privilege. This time, instead of walking into classrooms and praying over desks, I walked into each teacher's classroom and just listened.

I used to attend church with the sweetest lady. She was the preacher's wife but not your typical preacher's wife from when I was a kid. She was humble, a servant, yet vocal and not at all untouchable. She was very, very real. She would voice a prayer and then wait. In a room full of teens. Just sit in silence. Shane and I helped with the youth group at the time, and I remember peeking my eyes open and looking over at him, wondering if we shouldn't jump in and finish the prayer. But all she was doing was waiting for an answer. She would quietly resume her prayer when she felt she had heard what she needed to hear, and sometimes it wasn't what she wanted to hear. I know that in those moments, it taught those kids and me so much about the power of Christ, the power of prayer, and the power of faith. I can honestly say that in all of my years reaching out to God, I have seen signs and watched people swoop in and take care of my family during our worst nightmare, but he has never called an audible quite like I was hearing last Monday morning.

Teachers are hurting right now because not only are we serving students, but we feel strongly that we serve our communities. Some of our community members are not on board with the decisions made at the state department level, including the health department guidelines, which obviously trickle down to our public schools. The uncertainty of these times does not diminish the desire of a teacher to create an environment where students have the freedom to learn and discover safely. Teachers will do that no matter where they are. They want to be a part of the solution for families everywhere. They want to present their material, and they will work day and night to make it happen.

I am taking an online class from Yale University. Teachers are learners, and when I saw a free class from Yale, I wanted in! #1 because I could then add to my wall of fame a certificate from YALE!!! #2 Free!!! Yes, please! The professor is unbelievable and our principal, who introduced me to the course, now calls this professor her Buddha. "The lesson of much contemporary research in judgment and decision-making is that knowledge— at least in the form of our consciously accessible representation of a situation—is rarely the central factor controlling our behavior," Santos & Gendler (2014). In my terms, this suggests that when you react outwardly and socially to an issue that you perceive as a problem, you aren't reacting based on knowledge, but rather on your own feelings. Let's all check ourselves for a moment. We all do this. We are probably all guilty of assessing our feelings first and knowledge second when presented with an issue, but we don't all share our frustrations so publicly. I know opinions are free and that is a beautiful thing, but exactly how much of the negative/victim-level emotions are being gifted to our own children? Their burdens are heavy right now, too. I want to teach mine to overcome...anything. To tuck and roll. To seat, roll, and come up chopping (one football coach's advice for life based on an old drill, yet no one should be seated during this time). To adjust. To be bendy/flexible. To put egos aside. To recognize your blessings. To think through other's needs and what they might look like vs. your own. To imagine yourself helping someone accept this, and to not contribute to the negative pools that are forming everywhere.

I walked into the building last Monday morning nervous, lonely knowing that the students would not be with us, anxious for some of my school family who I knew would struggle learning new technology, and overwhelmed by the thoughts of my children not getting to be face to face in the nurturing environment of the classroom. Some teachers have even described their feelings as feelings of grief. Overall as a nation we could probably all describe the last 6 months in that way, but when you consider yourself a professional griever you know the difference. After a simple walk around the building, I felt that there was hope. I can take you through the grieving process and tell you there will be ups and downs, that every day will be different, and that the process is as unique as the person experiencing it. I can also tell you that grieving people can't 'fix' what they are grieving about, so this is where I believe there is a light. Although the global pandemic is still very much present, history would tell us that eventually it will be exactly that...a part of our history. We have the opportunity to fix our mindsets on the task at hand, which should be offering the next generation the ability to see adults who are problem solvers, strong and positive thinkers, people who refuse to respond as victims, and who support others despite their own opinions.

I could go on all day about the amount of work that was accomplished in one week of preparations for our 'pivot to home' program, which is set to start this year. It was astounding! This week, we will make sure all of our new friends have a personal device to get started and are greeted wide-eyed and with a smile behind our masks, while we hand out the technology gateways in a well-organized, yet hot parking lot pickup. I will leave you with some of the words that came to me loud and clear last week as I entered different classrooms:

Warrior

Overcomer

Worship

Speak Revival

Glory to God

Fresh

Renewal

Freedom

Power

Jesus, by the power of your spirit and the truth in your word, help us. Cover us. Claim our community as your own and comfort the parents, comfort the children, comfort the leaders who are tired, comfort the weary educators, and provoke a fire in us as we accept the challenge to rise above our own desires for simpler times. Help us to appreciate the gifts of others and recognize the needs we can serve in your name. And, Jesus, thank you for showing your face to me last week when my heart was broken by the words of others who had lost hope and needed someone to blame. Jesus, thank you for replacing the sadness in my heart with the words you spoke to me about my coworkers. Wow, just wow. More of you, less of me. Everyday. Amen.

*G.I. Joe Fallacy Santos & Gendler (2014).*
<u>*Knowing is half the battle?*</u> **Edge.org**

IT IS BECOMING HARDER TO FEEL
PRODUCTIVE AND HELPFUL
IN MY OWN HOME.

# Not a Burden, but a Blessing. Reflections of 2020...

12/31/20

Something about a year that is both epic, terrible, dreadful, life-changing, and memorable to the entire world, yet it became a year of forced reflection for me and so many others. I don't always see that as a bad thing. I am going to list both for my future self and for anyone who might need to hear it...My Top 10 Journal Entries for 2020. My brilliant and beautiful friend, Brandi, was photo journaling her girls throughout the quarantine and asked me if I was writing. I was indeed, but when someone asks you this, as they expect it from you, you tend to kick up the commitment. So, here are some excerpts from my Captain's Log - Corona 2020.

1.  I see how we've all made sacrifices and adjustments for each other now that we're doing life from home. I see a compassion

for finding spaces that are useful and meaningful. We attended 'Bedside Baptist' today as we have come to know it, we don't even attend a Baptist church, but it's catchy. Tate prayed for his friends in the foreign exchange program. It is a burden on his heart. They may not be able to make it home as planned. It amazes me what our children will worry about and remember from this time. It is crucial to support one another right now.

2.  In February, I began my master's program. I didn't tell anyone. After the Spring Break shutdown, my boys think I'm always doing classwork for my teaching job. It is much harder in that regard, as I am now attempting to keep 140 students engaged in an online platform they weren't trained to use, while motivating my own children to stay positive, and actually writing papers for my master's classes. I have bitten off a lot here. Finding refuge in having nowhere to really go. Being home and pouring myself into all of this...oh, and housework...oh, and teaching someone to drive...oh, and I have a senior!

3.  Today was hard. I am not going to lie. Found out that a lady I work with has been dealing with this virus. Her mom has been admitted to St. Francis, and it doesn't look good. It makes me so nervous and scared for her and her family. For all of us. We also found out today that there will most likely be no school the rest of the year. No prom. No graduation ceremony. No All-State game. No..No..No. It is a rough reality we are facing, and yet it seems so selfish to even be upset about it.

4.  It is becoming harder to feel productive and helpful in my own home. My boys are very independent and it can be lonely. Being a widow typically has zero advantages, but based on all of the griping about excessive togetherness and failed marriages

during this year, I guess I am supposed to count my lucky stars. Oy!

5.    March 25...Randy, my best friend's dad, who has been battling cancer, is coming home today. This is both a good and a bad thing, but was made possible by the compassion of the staff and therapists at his care facility, one of them being Teresa, Tate's girlfriend's mother. Heroes!!! The end is too near. Tate found out today that his high school season is officially over. He fields numerous calls throughout the day and receives texts from his teammates and friends who are losing their minds. He hasn't really had time to lose it himself. Kassidy came over, and so I made chocolate chip cookies and banana bread. Comfort foods for kids who don't generally even eat many sweets. We will get through it, but it is so hard for these kids to feel like they got cheated.

6.    Wyatt and I attended a send-off to honor a soldier who had fallen in Iraq. We grabbed breakfast (our first drive-thru experience) and waited on the side of 46th Street N by the base for him to come by. There were thousands of people. We stayed for hours and didn't care. He gave his life.

7.    Mandi texted me to tell me to come on out to see her dad if we wanted— Corona or no corona. I had a strong sense of unease about him all day. While I was there, his breathing almost stopped. Mandi, her mom, and her sister, Kendra, gathered around the bed and begged him to breathe. They hooked some oxygen back up, and we physically lifted him as high as we could in the bed. They asked me to call the hospice nurse for her to head back out and someone called Levi, Mandi's brother, to tell him to hurry. Chloe, Mandi's niece, teared up and

climbed into my lap, then Savana took her outside. As soon as I
knew the nurse was on her way and I checked on Chloe, I told
Chris I was going so the driveway would be clear for everyone and they could have their time. I prayed that Levi would
make it. I hadn't been home 20 minutes, and she let me know
that he was gone. Levi made it and he went peacefully. I am
left remembering just how he pushed his kids to be their best;
they pushed him and loved him enough to coach him through
breathing and waiting for Levi. I have witnessed something
today that I will never forget. True Love.

8.    Started distance learning on a Monday, 46 texts to families I
      hadn't heard from by Thursday. Being an elective teacher has
      often really seemed insignificant during this time, but the
      students who love creating and challenging their minds are
      keeping me going. I pray that teachers around the world know
      their worth. This situation is making it very hard. There are
      a huge number of people who love trying new things, having
      their students home, and supporting what their teachers are
      trying to accomplish from afar. Other parents are pulling their
      kids to alternative online platforms, calling teachers babysitters,
      criticizing the very lessons we plan because they hear us struggle
      to keep the entire class's attention while online. This pandemic
      would be a great time for a Facebook/social media break. My
      intentions are pure with my students, and I am pouring into
      them the best I know how at this very moment— loving them
      where they are, sending letters to their homes, and calling
      them. Whatever it takes to say hello, that I love them, and I'm
      thinking about them.

9.    In the last week, I have repaired a toilet seat, shower head, and
      planted a few flowers. The 7th grade teachers are participat-

ing in a step challenge with the 6th grade teachers, and I have walked well over 100,000+ steps in two weeks time. Waving at my new neighbor friends, whom I have never met until now. Yelling across the streets to each other while we get our exercise feels very Mayberry and nice. Wyatt got a new puppy finally. Her name is Annie, and she brings a new life around here. Potty training, keeping Willow from treating her like a toy, and watching her grow. She's a doll, and as much as he wanted a dog to sleep with him, she sleeps with me so far. I suppose I'm winning at life. He wasn't really into getting up in the middle of the night after all. We took a Covid road trip to Kansas to get her, and she's been worth every bit of the hype so far!

10. We are coming so close to the anniversary date, and I try not to dwell on it, but it's so hard not to. The days leading up to losing Shane were just so normal  We were loving life on the little Farley Farm and enjoying Spring there. We were getting in a real groove of happiness and contentment that our life was lacking through the years. I just can't deal sometimes. Then, as if she read my mind, my sweet friend, Elo, shows up with a card and some distance hugs. She loves my boys and me, and I am so grateful for friends who aren't afraid to acknowledge the hurt. Yesterday, I had my first ORU parent meeting! NUTS! Shane would be flipping out! I loved it.

I only made it to May, and my journaling slowed as we entered the end-of-school craziness. I will never share my journals from the beginning of the Fall semester when we found out we were back online. They mainly consist of trying to find a way to soften parents' hearts toward our administration for making that choice, and some include some not-so-nice things that were said to me in passing by parents. Words matter, people! Even when we are adults. So many other highlights:

Tate was part of an excellent graduation commencement speech, my little sister married a beautiful man on the side of a mountain in Arkansas, we pulled off a prom, my niece is pregnant with her 2nd girl, Lane tore his ACL and has battled out an epic suck of a year like a champ, Wyatt made the Jr. High golf team after deciding he was just going to go for it, my brother and family moved to Florida, my precious work son, Antonio, had his first child, I am now just a few classes away from having my masters and finally told the boys what the heck I was up to, Tate is living his dream and thriving with a 4.0 his first college semester and gearing up for soccer season number one as a college athlete, we had some amazing visitors when everyone thought it was safe, and we still managed to make it to Big Cedar once during this unprecedented time. We have fished, visited the museum as often as safely allowed, hiked, biked, walked, kayaked, golfed, baked, tried new recipes, and read amazing books! I survived my 20th wedding anniversary without my love and went out of town by myself to see some artwork in person just because I wanted to celebrate. I have a dream team of friends who will pray for the smallest of needs at a moment's notice, and together, we have made it! We have loved each other through it all and will continue to do the same. My prayer is that I never look back on this year and think it was in any way a burden, because when I read back over my journal pages, I realized it was the farthest thing from that. It was a blessing.

REAL AND HEARTSICK
BUT SLOWLY COMING UP FOR AIR.

# He Didn't Want to be a ****ing Tree

1/13/21

I went out back to the school forest after school to stand and stare at Shane's tree. I was thinking how 'tree' isn't even really the right word for it. My school family bought it for us and had it planted in his honor. I gathered the boys years ago and took a picture of them in front of it to commemorate its arrival and mark a baseline to watch it grow. Cue the confusion. Later that evening, I recall thinking, 'That isn't a redbud.' It's way too big already.

I am a science teacher for goodness' sake, and I am one of the teachers who manage that forest, and I should know what kind of tree it is, and it is NOT a redbud. The state tree of Oklahoma. The tree chosen as a beautiful way to remember Shane. Its heart-shaped leaves would be green all summer after a beautiful, dark pink spring budding. It was to be perfect.

The next day, I called the nursery that has been in our town for ages and which planted the tree. They immediately knew why I was calling, stating they had made a mistake. They would be coming to swap it out for the actual intended tree and deliver the existing tree to its rightful owners. This was already shaping up to be an interesting story and very much in the true Farley fashion of something never going quite right the first time.

A new tree was planted and promptly died, so we were hopeful that the third time's the charm moment that had always been the theme of our dating experience and marriage. Well, it wasn't, and I stood before a nearly totally dead tree that very day, thinking how last year as a whole felt terrible. One day, I had been so far beyond depressed and sunken into a hole that I recall getting out of my car and walking out of the garage to the mailbox when a giant branch off of our front yard tree decided to fall. If I had been under it, I would have been at the very least hospitalized. It was a real Holy Spirit moment of renewal and awakening. There was no wind, no storm brewing, no sign of a diseased or dying tree. It started cracking dramatically, so loudly that anyone nearby would have stopped to look, and it fell. Right in my path. Ok, God. I see you. I hear you. I need you. I will wake up and smell the coffee. I will regain focus on my children's needs and my self-worth. I will try to live outside of darkness and dread.

That day after school, as I looked at the sad redbud in what was left of its dormant winter state, anticipating spring, and knowing it was going to look terrible, I remembered that branch. I decided right then and there to grab life by the horns and yank that dern tag out of the ground that had his name on it. Take it home and put it on my own redbud someday. I yanked and twisted, cut my hand, cussed, and cried. Two of my friends came out to check on me and I told them that I had come to the conclusion that he didn't want to be a ****ing tree.

Some days my actions are just not something to be proud of, but if my boys had watched me walk through this moment, we may have all had a good laugh. Mom is losing it. Real and heartsick but slowly coming up for air.

REEXPERIENCE YOUR REFERENCE POINT.

# Please Join Me in Prayer
# A Widow's Guide to Valentine's

10/15/21

I am going to say this out loud. I predict a flipped school year in 2021-22. Who will understand what I mean? I hope everyone who has a child, owns a business, attends events, teaches children, coaches a team, runs a restaurant. Basically, I hope everyone will witness this revolution unfold alongside me. I am partly making this prediction for my own sanity and because I recently found a list of prayer requests that I had left on my desk sometime just past the middle of the last school year. This list would not make sense to share and may seem insignificant to many, but let me just say this: all three requests have been granted because God is so dang good!

Near this sticky note, I found another. It's a thing with me and my aging mind, something my grandmother has always done and I now do. Write nearly everything down. I wrote 'Reexperience your reference point'. Now, I wish I could remember where I first read that, what podcast I heard it on, or what brilliant person told me to do this? I found several references to it online, but I would like to give credit to Dr. Santos at Yale. Y'all, take the online class, read the book, read the author notes when you are tired and want to be done, because that is where the good stuff lives.

My prediction for the year is something I want to claim now. Pray over it with me, will you? Let's have an army of prayer warriors after this one!! As a middle school teacher, I have witnessed awkwardness. I know what it looks like and experience it daily. It is the age. The underdeveloped frontal lobe. The long, detailed story about something truly brilliant and intellectual they watched on YouTube and the little video game-inspired dance move they do when they walk away from you. The students I meet who have had to grow up too quickly and already don't know how to relax...to the one who always draws wolves and brings you homemade gifts from their bus stop. The Kardashian inspired girls and the boy who looks like a surfer, even though we live nowhere near a beach. I love them all! Well, this year, they are different.

In all fairness, we are all different. We have been living in the unknown. Shopping online, and now that some of us are back in the grocery store, we don't know how to act. Do we get close enough to hug a friend we've just run into, or is that allowed? We are walking around in invisible, unspoken social bubbles that have isolated us for the last year and a half, and we don't know what the reentry drill looks like. In the top-notch school where I teach, kids have lost their sense of what is acceptable, but haven't we all? I had to decide about a week ago that I was going to get out of the negative space in my head about it, despite the TikTok challenges unfolding right before my eyes. Yes, they are true. I have had property stolen right off my shelf behind my desk, a lovely penis made of the pipe cleaners we were using for a project left as a gift for me on someone's way out of my classroom (we witness a lot of male genitalia drawings but this little blatant gift drop off took... well, balls), we lost multiple soap dispensers in one week, kids don't seem to have a sense of spatial reasoning in the hallways, disrespect is off the charts, and I could list all of the other infractions. Still, it just starts to sound like we have no control and we have got the best of the best staff and administration. Despite the craziness, there has to be a silver lining.

Here is what the request entails. Pray with me and claim this. A flipped year! This springtime behavior we are witnessing is their reentry. The amount of brain development that would have occurred socially during the tightest of shutdown times will hopefully catch up, and the maturity and restraint they typically exhibit when school starts will be evident after Christmas. They will settle in. They will know their worth. They will know we care. They will let go of hostility and animosity from watching the news, hearing so many opinions that clash about who is doing things right or wrong in our world, and they will know they are in a safe place with people who love them. That they will feel supported and nurtured in the way school should feel. That we all normalize asking for mental support, asking questions, and trusting someone will take you seriously, and accepting that others may not have the same convictions and approaches to coping as you or your family is ok.

Revisiting the reference point of all that was wrong when this all started and realizing that we have had heroes all around us the whole time, and still do. People have lost so much love in their lives. Students have had to experience things most adults wouldn't have been made privy to when they were young. Grandparents have died alone. Adults have lost their jobs. Stability has been rocked. Children have been without contact with many adults or other children, and some are not in great situations to have been alone for such extended periods.

If I revisit my reference points for significant events in my life, I can always see where growth has occurred. I often see where growth can still happen. Socially, I am behind. I have a wonderful group of friends, but I only socialize with a few and not typically anywhere but via text or possibly during 2 minutes between classes when I get to visit with my neighbor teacher. We are all behind socially right now. I don't meet new people well. I have a real mic dropper of an introduction, especially when inevitably in some naturally scripted conversation written 1,000 years ago, someone asks what my husband does for a living, and people don't know how to respond so I usually avoid situations where I might meet anyone new.

I am not an Instagram influencer, and I am not familiar with the latest trends. I would like to initiate a movement of prayer in our community, focusing on giving others a break. Loving our kids' quirks and supporting their needs. Loving our regained freedoms and believing we will continue to see more open up. Not giving up on the squirrliest of students, neighbors, or store clerks. Showing patience with ourselves and others. As teachers, we often feel that we finally start to learn about the personalities and details of our students by Christmas. Let's use that to our advantage and love them more openly by simply attempting to connect with them. It will pay dividends, and I am thanking God in advance for what I know can happen as the year ends.

YOU DON'T KNOW YOUR OWN STRENGTH
UNTIL IT IS TESTED.

# Your Dad Would Just Be...

6/3/21

Your dad would just be: rolling his eyes, cracking up, slapping you silly, losing his mind, squeezing your neck, beaming with pride. This is an endless list. The number of times I have said those words in this last year alone is countless, and to some people, even annoying. I had someone tell me just yesterday that they don't talk about their deceased relative the way we talk about Shane. It is hard not to when these boys are all still young, and I am constantly channeling what we would have done together in any given situation, such as solving a problem, encouraging one of them, or discipline one of them when the times call for it. And, yes, if you are uncomfortable with hearing about my dead spouse...you might just be uncomfortable around me. No apologies for that. So, on what would have been our 21st wedding anniversary, I will break down the last year for my own records and in the hope that it will give someone a reason to smile today or a reason to realize that nothing is too big for God. He has equipped this family with the armor to hit just about anything head-on and take what gets thrown our way in stride.

This world has lost its ever-loving mind. The pandemic alone would have had him speechless. Masks, no masks. He would have fought wearing one on occasion, but certainly did what needed to be done to work, shop, and manage everyday life for his family. He would indeed have been rolling those green eyes at the number of obstacles a group of people can face in a short period of time, or at the next hurdle that would come our way. It's been a year for our family. A year of firsts for many globally, and a full, at times difficult year for us. One of the almost year-long, not-so-glamorous highlights was Lane tearing his ACL in the first official pre-season scrimmage of the year. In his full-length, pegleg brace, pre-MRI reading, pre-surgery, pre-leg bending machine for days on end, we had a neurology appointment that was scheduled for months. We didn't dare reschedule, as we had been awaiting any clues on how to manage some persistent migraines that Lane had been dealing with off and on for the past few years that had suddenly become very regular. Our pediatrician is the greatest! Super thorough and considers family history at every turn. We had done sugar testing, EKG and echos, blood pressure monitoring with and without, and even during workouts, food journaling, allergy treatment, sinus recauterized, the kid had been through it. None of these things were pointing in the right direction for any solution or cause. They examined his brain. It was still there (of course, a bad joke from his brothers and me) and showed no real issues. The neurologist drew a line straight back to his multiple concussions over the past few years. Sitting in this office with LJ, slated to be a varsity starter and breaking records left and right with pre-season lifting, yet about to have at least 6 months of rehab for his knee, and the doctor just told him he should never play football again.

The months that followed were dark. Could he still play and risk more permanent neurological damage? Yes, but this isn't an ACL. You only get one brain, and believe me when I say that a lot of well-meaning people have had a lot of opinions on our decision. The lack of impact alone has improved his daily symptoms, and that is enough for me. My friend recently finished a class or sports psychology and has a valid point. That starting in high school, there should be a sports psychologist on hand for students who have such devastating, career-ending injuries. If you are a non-sports person reading this, that may sound extreme, but taking away someone's 'identity' as an athlete and something they have loved since the 1st grade is no joke. They have to find themselves again. I am pleased to say that I feel we are finally making progress. The kid did virtual school, I was able to get him back with direct teacher instruction as soon as he was mobile, he fought COVID, quarantine from exposure, missing for physical therapy appointments, trying meds for migraines that backfired emotionally, and working through this loss of self that occurs when you lose a part of what you loved and enjoyed with your dad who is no longer here. Everything comes back to that. Shane would have known what to tell him, what to do, how to choose how far to push himself. Shane would also be proud of how he has handled it and how he has made new plans, new goals, and taken new opportunities in stride. My little sister, Emily, and her husband, Brandon, got him involved at their CrossFit gym. The support from that community has meant the world to me for Lane. There were bribes/rewards in the form of a new tattoo, which was not my idea (Tate's), but certainly motivated him to keep pushing through the first semester alone, and I know he will continue to break records. He has always been so mature, and his calm spirit has gotten me through some rough days. I get so excited to see where God takes Lane and how He will use all that he has learned about life in this last year. He gets stronger every day, in every sense of the word.

Some other notable highlights...we ALL had COVID. We were so short on substitutes when I had it that I would be teaching from home, while teachers on their planning times monitored my class in session while I was on the screens with the kids. Educators are amazing people. We all made it through by helping each other every step of the way, all year long. Nervous about coverage and the state of the world, I then put off a surgery until summer that I should have had over Christmas break, only to drive myself to the ER during a snow day because I was convinced that my insides were falling out. The surgery could no longer be ignored, and with just a few weeks until Spring break, they scheduled a total hysterectomy. What was sometimes a 6-week recovery was negotiated down to 3 as long as I behaved. I needed to be with my students, as I only have them for such a short time, and STEM is not conducive to subs, especially when in short supply. It is a lot to ask of someone when it is project based and full of hammers, duct tape, hot glue, etc. Again, thanks to my sister and the help of countless teachers and our principals, a handwritten note from me was delivered to a student I was concerned about, dinners were brought from even the very substitute that was saving my year, and my household ran like clockwork thanks to grocery store trips by my teen drivers and our new favorite friend...DoorDash!

Tate started college and had a successful year one. Upon moving in, we found out that his roommate had recently been diagnosed with diabetes. His mom went through a list of, if this happens, do this, and the final item was, 'if none of that is working, start chest compressions and call 911'. Well, Aunt Ashley was helping us move him in, and we left there with her beside herself. I was trying to process the actual drop-off of my child at school and the fact that he would be very responsible for someone else all at once, plus try to train for soccer and make good grades. She was ready to call the dean of housing and get him a new assignment. I told her I would see how he was feeling about all of this later in the day.

PTSD is a very real disorder. It is not just reserved for soldiers, but it certainly makes the most sense when describing situations that a soldier or first responder might encounter. Tate is the one who dialed 911 for his dad. He spoke with them and took their advice. He managed to call me and allow me to talk to Lane and Wyatt while he monitored the situation until the paramedics and I arrived at the house. Does he have PTSD? Certainly. Did he tell me that he was meant to be with his new roommate because God knows he might be the one who could handle it best? Certainly did. All I could do was cry and tell him that he was more mature than his aunt and I put together, and thanked him for being this type of example to me. You don't know your own strength until it is tested. A student once told me that I handled emergencies well...our emergency at the time was a hedgehog getting stuck under the classroom sink. I explained that I had been through worse, so this seemed like a breeze. I am encouraged daily by the moments when I want to say... "Oh, helllllllll naw" and my boys just say... "Bring it!"

Kids are cruel. So are adults, but thirteen-year-old boys in a group can be cruel. Wyatt had been acting a little off for a week or so, and then finally broke it down for me. A few boys had been teasing him. And when kids tease, it's like they don't have a ceiling. Nothing is off limits. I won't get into the details, aside from me visualizing the fight scene from Happy Gilmore with Bob Barker, because that was what I was going to do with these kids. Again, grace wins. He was going to prove them wrong by working harder than ever and improving every day so there was no more room to talk. He is following his own path to greatness and it doesn't include letting others define him or get in his way. He is both compassionate for others in need and passionate about what he wants. He is a sponge for knowledge, and when he's not wowing us with his understanding of the hierarchy of other cultures, he's studying and perfecting his next endeavor. He is a little old man and a teenager all wrapped up in a package that is changing a little every day.

This year has also brought hardships on several of my dearest friends. One lost her dad, another's husband is a COVID survivor after weeks on the ventilator, another's husband has bladder cancer and is fighting for his/their new normal. There is a helpless feeling as a friend when all you can do is pray, but I have learned not to look at it this way. There is no shame in that 'all', because it is no small task. Prayer in itself is an action and a creation of movement and for years I am sure that many of my friends were worried that they were not doing enough for me, when they were doing everything by praying. I have continued to witness Christ move mountains through prayer. If you read the text thread from my group of close friends alone, you would read answered prayers almost daily. Tangible proof that there is a God who tends his sheep and that bringing your requests to him is not a small thing. Philippians 4:6 tells us to do that exact thing AND to not be anxious!

I recently read Dolly Parton's autobiographical book "My Life in Lyrics". She speaks about writing as her form of God-space. She feels closest to him when she is writing and in times of trouble and darkness she said, "I go to that God core inside me. Even when I feel like my little pilot light might have gone out, I know it's still there. I just have to reignite it through prayer, faith, love, friends, and family." After reading her book, I was inspired. I haven't donated millions or started libraries. I haven't written countless songs that tell stories, but I do think we could all relate to that pilot light. This year, a lot of people's lights dimmed but I believe it is time to strengthen our faith and move forward like never before. I am grateful for the legacy that Shane left for his boys and I am thankful for the continual glimpses of him I get from these boys every day. I will never not be sad about his passing and I don't believe there is an expiration date on grief. I believe that with each passing year, there is a deeper longing for his presence but also a deeper understanding of what life looks like without him physically in it.

# Tattoos

I blame you, Shane. Period.

You were covered in them.

Talking me into a 'quick' stop on several vacations, and me, refusing to join you.

Once, even sacrificing a debit card to the ATM monster when cash was needed ASAP and you left the card in the machine… leaving us with no way to obtain money the rest of the trip. This was always our luck.

After your passing, my friends made an appointment. Leslie, telling the artist that we were not like his normal clientele. His response, "CLEARLY!" We all just laughed and watched the Sopranos with him on his laptop while he stabbed me repeatedly and I wished I was screaming the same expletives they were voicing on the show.

I fell in love. With Sarah's artwork, the support I was bathed in, and the permanent reminder of our new family verse.

My boys' wheels started turning.

By 15, Tate was beginning college visits. He trained with the team the night we arrived. Different state, very conservative university, and different tattoo regulations. We drove 45 minutes after training, birth certificate and notarized release in hand. It's good to know a notary, thanks Jenny. I watched over my shoulder, fully anxiety riddled and believing that DHS would bust through any moment. He stepped up to the plate and Shane's signature will forever be by his side. We toured university the next morning and he frequently dipped into the restroom to reapply post tattoo ointment and stare at it.

Lane, 14. A one day trip to Branson, where a dreadlocked, rastafarian tattooed the same prize over his heart.

Wyatt, 15, and by then Lane had found a favorite artist in Arkansas. We arrived with the same protocol and his bicep now houses his name housed in the outline of a guitar.

Everyone survived these outings without jail time and with memories made. That's really the point. Memories made that are actual keepers. New memories out of old hurts. Pain that can be reversed or even pain that can be leaned into when you need to take a peek at the reason you are the way you are.

WE ARE STILL NEVER ON THE SAME PAGE
ON THE SAME DAY, SO A ROLLERCOASTER
ENSUES FOR ME.

# Stay

7/26/22

'So fast these moments fade,' it's as if Matt Rollings wrote this for me, but I can't put this song in only one category according to where I need it most in my life. Just when I think my tears have all dried, my soul is emotionless, or my mind has numbed to allowing memories to live...I come back to Shane's playlists. Wyatt has picked up the guitar in the last 6 months, and these are the songs he gravitates toward. I will sit at the top of the stairs and listen to him practice in his room. I could do this for hours. He and Lane played together the other night and it was my favorite day in a long time.

You see, I am hitting an avalanche of milestones with my boys. Tate turned 21 yesterday, Lane turned 18, Wyatt is entering high school, and Lane is now a senior. Tate is a junior in college, for goodness' sake. I know there are days when they need advice straight from Dad. These are big moments. It is my understanding that this song was originally written as a ballad connecting parent and child. It is the most tender in this sense and could not be more true in every line.

This song also reminds me of my husband's legacy. Today is his birthday. He would have been 49. FORTY-NINE. He didn't have the opportunity to reach that next milestone on Earth. Many people react to us differently now, and all that I have read on the subject of grief points to this. It's been 7.5 years, so we should be getting used to it, moving forward, and getting over it. 'I'll always be the home you come back to in your heart'. You never get over it.

My boys are thriving, and what no one sees are the days when none of us are. They still happen, and I can be thankful that it's not as often. We are still never on the same page on the same day, so a rollercoaster ensues for me. I have learned to give myself a break on trying to fix every detail of every emotion and we just try to ride them out together. I will be forever grateful for their willingness even just to text me, 'Mom, I am struggling today.' They know they are free to struggle and sometimes I can see it in their eyes 'telling me what words can't say'.

So, if you have children, step-children, grandchildren, a love in your life, a lost love, a parent, a hurting friend or neighbor, a sick friend, a best friend, or _____ (fill in the blank where this song can bless your life). I hope this song hits for you. My friend lost his mother to Alzheimer's and can picture his dad in this line 'I will carry you until it's time to go'. It breaks my heart, but I have learned that sometimes you need to sit with your broken heart to see how hard it can push you to love more deeply. Who will you carry until it's time to go?

Matt Rollings is a genius. He knew precisely who would sing this song best. If you're not a current fan, I hope this inspires you to check him out and discover all that he has accomplished. He has a servant's heart for the musicians he accompanies and writes for, and that list is long and impressive. His dedication is so inspiring to me. Happy Birthday Shane! We miss you.

# Guitar Gains

Grandpa had the goods.

A '76 Alvarez Yairi.

The wood - perfect.

The pearl inlay - perfect.

The sound - priceless.

He is who taught Shane how to play.

He was a bluegrass picker and worked the cotton fields during the Great Depressions, so we all listened as he strummed around and told plenty of stories.

The years flew past and the trembling became too much for the Alvarez to hide.

He began asking Shane to play for him.

I knew we had to end up with that guitar.

I sat grandpa down and told him to name his price.

A man who didn't believe in the safety of the FDIC.

A man who believed your money was tracked by flying sensors, long before those were called drones.

A man who wrapped his earnings in tin foil and put them in a clothes hamper in the closet each time he got paid, then covered it with folded towels.

I knew this negotiation would be a chore, and I had to be ready to pay up quickly.

Fast forward to debts paid and guitar in hand.

Grandpa enjoyed seeing Shane play gigs with this family treasure for several years.

He would sit still with his pearl snap shirt and US Navy Veteran hat perched up high on his little head, his fingers drumming the nearest table or arm of the chair.

Grandpa is gone now.

He went after Shane and at that point, we struggled through the conversation of losing him over and over and over again when he wanted to talk about it.

He was, as grandpa would say, one of his best friends. The top of the corn!

Shane played that Yairi everywhere he went.

He had a few other guitars in the early days of playing. All wonderful, but none originally belonging to Marvin Franklin.

The boys cherish that guitar.

They play it occasionally but want to preserve the memory of their dad making it come to life.

Lane and Shane had a plan on our land to breed show quality lambs for the local FFA students. Lane, 9 at the time, worked tirelessly with our neighbor's horses to save for this venture. Our fence was complete and the barn was just about to get flooring when we lost his business partner. He took his earnings and bought an Alvarez. Fast Car was the first song he learned. A crowd favorite when Shane was playing anywhere.

A few years after teaching himself to play, Wyatt wanted a vintage Alvarez of his own.

One day, he was watching a youtube video about restoring vintage Yairis and Lane walked through the room. 'Hey, why are you watching Rusty's neighbor??'

Wyatt laughed and said that it was just a random guy on Youtube.

Indeed, it was someone in our hometown.

Restoring Yairi guitars.

We see you, God!

We went to visit him, Wyatt played the guitar on his back porch on a hot, summer night, and Wyatt used every penny of savings to purchase a Yairi just two years older than Marvin's original. It was made the same year I was born.

Musical talent is passed down generationally…genetically even.

So is grit.

So is dreaming big.

May the music never fade.

GRIEF JUST NEVER ENDS.

# My Future Self

6/13/23

Will there be regrets? Instant!

I have been a widow for eight years and almost two months now. We have moved twice and these tubs have moved with us. I remember packing them up when we first decided to move from what would have been our FOREVER home. Where we were going to spoil our grandkids with rides down to the pond, homemade ice cream, fishing, riding horses, petting sheep, collecting eggs, and just anything else we dreamed up for that amazing place. It's where we would have parked the RV that we were going to travel to bluegrass festivals in when we both retired. It is also where it was too much. Too much to care for on my own with a 13, 10, and 7-year-old.

I packed these tubs because I couldn't bear to say goodbye to the contents. The things that had once touched his skin. These things he had sweat in to make a living for his family and create a beautiful life for us. These things he had worn to weddings he didn't want to attend and parties he would pretend to not be the life of. These pieces of cotton that had once held me tight and rocked our boys to sleep. These swim trunks we had taken to Big Cedar, where he tried stand-up paddle boarding to show Tate it was safe. Even the kind of socks he loved still matched up and ready to go.

As I type this, they are on the curb. Ready for the American Veterans to come and rescue. To take them to a place where someone else will love them before they turn into moth-speckled, old rags. Did I go back through every piece just now? Yes. Do I have too many things to hang in my closet for 'just in case' the boys may want them or I may want just to snuggle up and cry? Yes! We have the most beautiful keepsake quilts and pillows, made by the hands of those who love us...my stepmom and my CC. His jeans are now scattered all over my house in different ways. So, why do I want to run out and drag these back into the garage?

Grief just never ends. That is why. I am praying that my boys will know that I felt strong today. I felt like I could let these things go to a new home. They have witnessed me open and close these tubs for years now. I always say it's not quite time. I have shed many tears over how to handle my grief, their grief, the grief of his mother and father, my family, and his friends who love him so much. I know in my heart that I can't fix everyone's hurts, but I sure wish I could. Knowing he would have thrown them out long ago should help me. Knowing he is probably shaking his head every time I am upset. He is probably wishing I would suck it up already.

Maybe one person who reads this will feel normal. Anyone grieving a loss of any kind or feeling lost in this world. I have come to realize that loneliness isn't just for the broken-hearted. If you are ever feeling overwhelmed and need someone to pray for you or if you want to talk, please reach out! My friend called me crying, and she was sitting in her closet, wondering what she was supposed to do with her husband's things. I had to tell her that 8 years later, I still do not know the correct answer. We have to do what is right for ourselves and our family.

I just told a friend last night that the only peace I have truly found in this season of my life has been through watching God work. Miracles on miracles, including giving me the strength to let go of 4 tubs. I want my future self to remember that when she feels down, alone, and defeated...SHE WILL NEVER BE.

Here's hoping the AMVETS have made it by when I go outside.

# Share Your Story

12/2023

Law school is on the horizon for my oldest. He has had to reflect deeply and write a personal statement for some of the schools where he is applying. It is very difficult to express answers to some of the questions that they ask. I have always encouraged the boys to be as honest as possible. With his permission, here was a portion of a required entry he submitted.

## Statement of Unique Perspective by Tate Farley

For the first thirteen years of my life, everything was perfect. I had a loving family, a great group of friends, and was relatively successful in all of my endeavors. Then my dad died. He had a sudden heart attack while on the phone with my soccer coach at the time. Being the nosey thirteen-year-old I was, I was at the foot of his bed listening to every word of their conversation. This gave me a front row seat to my dad collapsing off of his bed and onto the floor as his heart ceased to function. My two younger brothers rushed into the room as I attempted CPR and anxiously called an ambulance and then my mother to alert her of the situation. That was the last time I saw my dad.

Since then, the events of that night have replayed themselves in my brain at unpredictable times. I have lived with PTSD and Generalized Anxiety Disorder for nine years now. For years I holistically blamed myself and was convinced that if I were more of a man I could have saved him that night and made life for my mom and my brothers insurmountably better. I now accept that some things are completely out of our control and I am thankful for the childhood I had both before and after my dad's death. Seeing how God has used this tragedy in my family's life to help so many others through the efforts of my mom, myself, and my brothers has been a great blessing.

Growing up in a single parent household while battling PTSD was no cake walk, but I believe it has given me a unique perspective on life and service that I will take with me into Law School. These obstacles have shown me the importance of resilience, compassion, and teamwork. I cannot imagine where I would be without the support system my family has had, the resilience of my mom that she has passed on to me, and the compassion we have received from the Lord and others.

Most importantly, this tragedy taught me that there is no sense in wasting time in life. It is my dream to graduate from Law School and make a difference in this community through service. It would be a disservice to the work of my father, my mother, and the talents the Lord has blessed me with if I did not go after this goal wholeheartedly. I believe that my perspective gained from these events makes me a unique candidate for Law School and will one day help me become a successful lawyer.

# Cowboy Chris and the Martin

Another guitar miracle happened.

Uncle Chris, the cowboy, accomplished the unthinkable.

Not only is he our on-call electrician and golf scramble organizer, he still picks and grins with the best of them.

He tracked down and convinced a nomadic dreamer to resell his old guitar back to him.

A Martin, originally owned by Shane.

This will now be in the hands of my boys whenever they want to play it…forever.

The placement of individuals in our lives never ceases to renew my faith and dig me out of the deepest, darkest holes of hurt.

THESE ARE MOMENTS TO REJOICE.

# Growing Pains and More Reality

2/2024

My youngest is enrolling in his Junior year in high school. He drives in a month. My thoughts on this are so daunting. He was only 7 when Shane passed, and he is his twin. I am not worried about him driving; I am worried that his car will never get too far from the driveway. I want him to experience life, but I adore the fact that he is a creature of habit who finds comfort at home. Golf, guitar, shower, rinse, repeat.

My middle son spent an entire year post-high school graduation in preparation to join the fire department. He has his final interviews coming up to find out if he's in or not. He would be the youngest to join this academy class. He is strong and capable. He became an EMT and completed all of his ride-alongs to prepare for the testing. He passed and is so ready to start his career.

My oldest was accepted to multiple schools and started the law school of his choice in January. He is the youngest in his class as well. He is considered a ½ L, meaning he started in the middle of a year. He graduated with his undergrad a semester early and had already passed the LSAT, so he decided to go for it. He received over ½ of his tuition in scholarships, and I could not be happier about that. These are moments to rejoice. They are moments that parents wait all of their lives to celebrate! Sometimes we don't get it all right. I know I haven't. Tate still gets lost while taking a jog in our neighborhood. He can't always find his way and ends up running in circles without the help of his GPS. Lane still gets the giggles when I get onto him about the slightest thing, so I pray his academy goes well. My sweet Wyatt wants to do anything but be at school. He will start concurrent enrollment with our local junior college and be a full year into his degree by the time he starts at a university. He likes to fast-track life, nothing wrong with this but I really want him to enjoy the journey.

THIS WASN'T HIS PATH AND
GOD KNOWS WHAT'S TO COME.

# Just a Few Months Later

I started the previous entry and walked away from it. I got sidetracked with who knows what at the time, but much has changed. Lane got accepted and started the academy on an early Spring morning. All suited up, new lunchbox in hand, and full of nerves. Much like his first day of kindergarten, when my brave boy had to have a sweet lady named Mrs. Hester walk him to class so mommy could meet my own students.

Around 9 am on the first day of the academy, Lane messaged me. I couldn't believe it, as they were not even allowed to keep their phones. I asked if he was on a break and how it was going. He told me not to freak out, and I was not allowed to come to meet him right away, but he had been taken to the ER. His precious girlfriend had just joined me at the state golf tournament, she had the day off and both of us needed to busy our minds while he had his big first day. She graciously offered to stay at the tournament to keep me updated on Wyatt so that I could go be with Lane. This is the type of girl the Lord has put in his path.

Selfless and caring. Tate had a rare early out day at school and joined in supporting Wyatt while waiting for news on Lane.

Lane, my kid who has had a multitude of rare things happen to him medically, was admitted to the neurological ICU for observation. They determined that he had a mini-stroke. They found a slight thrombosis in his sinuses that could have caused it, but to say he was devastated is not even close to the sadness he was feeling. We all were.

We spent two days and almost two nights there. He was cleared after every test one's brain can possibly have, as well as cardio testing. The Neurologist on duty wrote a letter stating that he would allow him back with no hesitation, but sadly, the fire department didn't share the same sentiment. Understandably, as this event was now considered a liability risk, and they would need about five years of clear medical records before allowing him to continue.

An entire year wasted, in his opinion. Devastated and broken, he didn't speak much at all for almost two weeks. He quietly recovered, and I prayed. Begging God that he knew his worth and that he would be ok. This wasn't his path and God knows what's to come. All of these right and true things that come to mind to say at a time like this are much like what people say to a grieving family member—and are not well received. We just had to give it time, and it will forever be a part of his story.

My boys have been through things others would never dream of enduring. It is very hard for someone to hear that things will work out exactly the way they are supposed to when a dream is shattered, but we know this to be true. God's manning the ship. I have this quote hanging in my classroom, "A ship in a harbor is safe, but that's not what ships are built for." That is often attributed to Admiral Grace Hopper, a woman who blazed a trail of programming in a time when few women served our country and certainly not in that role. Just when we think we have our safe harbor, we may need to get back out there and sail.

HE CARES FOR ME SO WELL.

# High Fives & the Grace of God

2/20/25

There is an entry in this book that talks about our friend who went through an awful divorce. We were in his wedding party, went on their first date with them, and celebrated the birth of their children, birthdays, etc. This man is a friend who has never not been in my life, grew up in my same church, was my brother's college roommate, and sang gig after gig with my husband. They were the best of friends. He says that his goal was always to create the right platform for Shane's voice. They got each other and could talk for hours. They each had a respect for what the other brought to the table musically and they made a great team. They even once nearly named their band, 'No, We're Not Brothers' because of how many times they were asked this question.

I decided to take myself to see Lyle Lovett at the Broken Arrow Performing Arts Center in October of 2016, knowing that this would need to be one of those hurdles that I jumped to allow myself to live a little again. I was only gone a few hours. I cried all the way there and off and on throughout the concert. At intermission, I looked around and noticed a lot of the same people who would come to his and Shane's shows were there, sprinkled in the crowd. A few said hi to me, seeming a little surprised to see me. I wondered if they knew how hard it was to come alone. I walked out to the lobby to find a restroom, and there he was with his father-in-law. I asked about his family and just like people describe how Shane would light up for the opportunity to talk about us, he did the same for his wife and kids. A community of music lovers and it was like God was telling me that everywhere I go, He was covering me with help if I needed it. Friends and encouragers who even with a wave could make me feel like I was in a safe place to listen and remember.

Just two months later, he was loading his kids in the truck in my driveway without the help of his wife. I had just asked his daughter if her mommy was still getting ready at her grandma and grandpas. He had stopped by for our kids to exchange Christmas gifts like we had their whole lives. Fast forward a few weeks later, when his wife called me to tell me she had found her 'soulmate' and I would understand her needing to live for today, as tomorrow is never promised. I explained that I didn't appreciate the comparison of her leaving her sweet husband and me losing mine. She and I haven't spoken since. He tried everything to get her to reconcile. I prayed for them through this, as did many of our friends. She never came around and he was broken.

For the eight years that followed, we kept checking in with one another. We always had hilarious childhood connections like knowing all of the hymn numbers and the songs that correlated. Wondering where the 3rd verse of said songs went, as our church only sang 1st, 2nd, and last verses for some odd reason. Our spouses weren't raised in the same church as us, and we could joke about the strictness of the church. We are recovering Baptists and not afraid to discuss it. Our conversations over the years consisted of making sure the other was functioning as a human and not a zombie. We've talked about kids mostly and music, and teased each other about getting ourselves back out there.

He has been a solid friend to me since he came to my house the first time to play music in the early 2000's. He is one of the most genuine people I know. Honest to the core. He has supported my boys for years and encouraged them. When the boys finally came to grips with the strings needing changed on Shane's guitar for the first time after his passing, they wanted him to do it. He would be the only choice for the job. We saved them and put them in a shadow box. One of the last things we knew his hands had touched.

Through the years, concerts would come up and we would run into each other there. Once, we had both taken our kids to a concert an hour from each of our homes and didn't even know the other was coming. His mom got very sick and I felt horrible being too far away to be of any assistance. I felt like he was taking so much on and still in a fragile state. She passed way too soon. I attended the viewing and my oldest and I attended the funeral. Have you ever attended a funeral and only had your eye on one person there? I was so concerned with only my friend. My heart was breaking all over for him. His mom was a dream. She was perfect. I have visited her grave for years on his behalf since I am closer in proximity to the site.

We had always exchanged gifts for Christmas as well. I once got him a C.S. Lewis live reenactment experience. He got me the nicest pair of headphones that he knew I would never buy myself. While Tate finished his undergrad, he was just a few miles from his house. He became Tate's Amazon delivery drop to avoid it being lost at school and would occasionally leave him an envelope under the mat for a coffee run on him. He would show up for Tate's college games, Wyatt's golf, and whatever else he and the kids could make it to if we were in town. All the while, I would encourage him to put himself on Farmersonly. com or something equally as kitschy, knowing he would be too apprehensive to do so. He is a catch and some girl was missing out!

Last summer, he had offered his home for Wyatt and I to house-sit while he was out of town for work and we were in town for a golf tournament. This was a huge blessing! The volume of golf travel is high and the cost gets out of control. When I arrived, I noticed some vintage jars in his room filled with fresh flowers. I immediately had to tease him by taking a picture and sending him a text asking if his housekeepers would leave him fresh flowers. No response, which I wasn't concerned about because he was in meetings. We had been there a few days and made ourselves right at home. I had put a roast in the crockpot one morning, and we had finished our early round at the course. I was reading a book in the pool and Wyatt had gone to practice. He came back early and I of course was almost embarrassed. I offered for us to get a hotel and he insisted we stay. I then invited him to dinner in his own home. After dinner, Wyatt said he was going to bed because he knew we would 'talk for 6 hours'. We have always had the best conversations —nerds by nature and plenty of topics to explore.

That night, he asked me, as he had many times over the years, if I was ready to put myself out there and date again. This has now been nearly a decade for me. A decade of hurt, stress, and lost love. A decade of raising boys and chasing sports, of attempting to keep a household together alone, and of battling all of the depression and anxiety that grief brings. A decade of highs and lows, of waves crashing.

Him: Are you ready?

Me: No, it sounds like too much worry and work. I think I'm good. Why? Are you ready for me to set you up a farmersonly?

Him: No, but what about us?

Me (jaw hitting the floor): Precious MAN, are you asking me out?

Eight months later, we see each other no less than once a week and we are an hour and a half apart. My boys could not be happier. I waited a month to tell them, and they all responded almost exactly the same... only he would do. He and I have talked so much about Shane and that he might just be high-fiving him about now. I knew it was right when he explained that he had known he wanted to take care of me for a long time. He had prayed, read, and researched how to properly date a widow and he knows I will need space sometimes and the boys will always need support. He cares for me so well.

He makes me feel like a priority and he desires for me to be free from pressure and worry. He loves me for being unapologetically me and wants me to feel protected. Tom Petty describes a kind of freedom that I finally feel in his song Wildflowers. He wants me to feel free, close to him, able to be protected and taken care of, without worry or trouble. In his mind, it's that simple.

We have compiled a playlist of well over 100 songs that speak to us about each other. I haven't smiled this much in a decade, and I was honestly so surprised that my butterflies were not dead. He encourages me to do things that make me happy. We enjoy art and cooking, travel, and could sit for hours...maybe days on the patio and talk. We talk about how perfectly timed our relationship has been and how we have always understood each other. One of his friends told me that his core group of friends thinks he has loved me for a very long time. I am so happy that we both recognize the value we bring to each other's lives.

I wrote a prayer for our relationship after that very weekend and have prayed it every morning. Sanctify us, Lord! May our first priority always be the hearts and raising of our children. He is a wonderful man of God, a breath of fresh air, and a gift. Losing a spouse often means that conversations were not had about the what-ifs. What if I pass? Would you date someone else? Some couples have the difficult opportunity of discussing this during a long illness, but regardless, I did not think it would ever be easy to allow yourself to love again. I used to tease my friends who would ask me about dating that God would have to send a man to my door to knock and say, "The Lord sent me to take you to dinner" in order for me to know it was ok. BUT GOD. I have never understood this phrase like I do today...but God. He redeems our stories for His glory. He provides. He manifests our happiness under His guidance and in His time.

God's grace surpasses all boundaries. It is good every time. It is freely given and rich when you are poor. It is calm when there is chaos. Grace wins. None of us are perfect but we are perfectly suited and equipped by Christ to care for others. I appreciate my entire network of friends and family for all they have done for my boys and I. For the special care and consideration they have always given and for their attempt to never further upset us. To handle every situation with care.

My journey to hope continues but I can see the outline of a life that has been God-breathed and despite the heartache, I will be forever grateful for the opportunity to have seen his glorious miracles and majesty at work.

By the way, those flowers were for me.

# ACKNOWLEDGMENTS

Thank you to my boys for being the best copilots in life. I love the way you see each other for who you are as individuals. Thank you for being the best example for me along the way. Being your mother is my greatest accomplishment!

Thank you to my siblings for loving and pushing and encouraging me. I know we have our own story and that is for another book and another day. You are one of the most talented groups of functioning adults I know! I love you!

To my parents, our story wasn't tidy, and our tree grew in unexpected directions, but it still gave me the ground I stood on and the wind I chased. Thank you for giving us life and space to grow. Love you!

To Shane's parents, The loss of a son is a sorrow I can't imagine putting into words—but when it comes without warning, it strikes with a cruelty that shatters time itself. Thank you for continuing to love our boys. In the shadow of grief, you have helped carry forward his legacy with grace, and for that, I am deeply grateful.

Thank you, Matt Moffett, for opening your studio to me when creativity was my only safe place. I was actually just there for the advice and laughs. I'm not sure you will ever know what you did for me. Go Rams!

Thank you to my Bunco girls who prayed while Ashley ran me to meet the ambulance and have continued to be by my side through our entire journey.

Thank you to my "Creative team" who have always thought more of me than I have of myself. We have all absolutely been through the wringer and came out smiling because of each other.

Amber and the Sarahs, may I always be able to pay you in mangoes and have a seltzer at noon! Artists are truly people who look for the good and I have learned so much from each of you. You are all three celebrities to me!

AG, my 4th son, who God sent straight to the O7GC to be a light to so many, but mostly to bring realness and love to my boys! Thank you for inspiring so many with your own story.

The Everetts, thank you for being our family and loving us and always being a phone call away... even if it was just for changing light bulbs!

Chris Hughes, your compassion for my boys is never-ending. Thank you!

Nekki, my sister, loss has changed us both but love and grace will sustain us!

Tommy Wheeler, my kindred spirit in raising kids and dealing with loss. Thank you for telling me on the sidelines of a football game that I was not allowed to stay mad...at Shane or Tommie. Tough love lasts!

Lindsey Hogan - protector of hurting hearts, always willing to remove your earrings and go toe-to-toe for a friend. May we all strive to be more like you!

Jared Tyler, Norway's timing still reminds me of the beauty of his life. Thank you for your friendship. Your talent is unmatched!

To all of the coaches and teachers who have impacted the lives of my boys, you deserve a parade in your honor! They would not be the men they are without you.

To all of the sports mommas and daddies…sideline siblings and grandparents who have cheered on my boys. The Lord has put people in our path, mentors and friends who have become family. We will never forget all of the extra love you have given us!

To Ryder Barnes, Fly High sweet angel. You have touched us all and I can only imagine that Shane is enjoying your laughter right now. You are his favorite kind of kid. Tough and tender. Your family has gone through a lot and taught us all how to fight.

Bestie Jenny from the Block, your penpal skills have saved my mental game more days than you know. Junk journals and coffee for life!

Thank you, B! What began in heartbreak for us both has become something healing and real—thank you for walking this path with me. I feel beautiful and free again, all thanks to you.

Thank you, Jesus, for carefully orchestrating this life of mine. May the music never fade.

# SUGGESTIONS & CREDITS

www.chicsparrow.com

www.littlemountainbindery.com

www.maydesigns.com

Buddy Owens
    Paintings - www.backstagenashville.net/buddyowens
    Instagram: @buddyowenspaintings

Chloe Wall Photography - Edmond, OK
A lifestyle photographer who graciously captured Shane's guitar. She is a gift and has an incredible eye for details. She works primarily in Oklahoma but is willing to travel. Her wedding photos are divine!

Emily Hill Photography - Owasso, OK
After watching our oldest sister capture this town's special moments for two decades, little sister accepts the challenge and is killin' it! I am pretty sure my last photo session without family was my bridal session moons ago and she made my author shots easy and enjoyable.

You can find a companion journal to this book on Amazon.

# Psalm 91
## A Psalm of Protection

Whoever dwells in the shelter of the Most High
    will rest in the shadow of the Almighty.

I will say of the Lord, "He is my refuge and my fortress,
    my God, in whom I trust."

Surely he will save you
    from the fowler's snare
    and from the deadly pestilence.

He will cover you with his feathers,
    and under his wings you will find refuge;
    his faithfulness will be your shield and rampart.

You will not fear the terror of night,
    nor the arrow that flies by day,

nor the pestilence that stalks in the darkness,
    nor the plague that destroys at midday.

A thousand may fall at your side,
    ten thousand at your right hand,
    but it will not come near you.

You will only observe with your eyes
    and see the punishment of the wicked.

If you say, "The Lord is my refuge,"
    and you make the Most High your dwelling,

no harm will overtake you,
    no disaster will come near your tent.

For he will command his angels concerning you
    to guard you in all your ways;

they will lift you up in their hands,
    so that you will not strike your foot against a stone.

You will tread on the lion and the cobra;
    you will trample the great lion and the serpent.

"Because he loves me," says the Lord, "I will rescue him;
    I will protect him, for he acknowledges my name.

He will call on me, and I will answer him;
    I will be with him in trouble,
    I will deliver him and honor him.

With long life I will satisfy him
    and show him my salvation."

*Dear Gracious Lord,*

*Please let at least one person be helped by reading this book. Bless the readers with the freedom to feel, the power to share, and the presence of mind to accept the grace you are offering. Thank you for your protection and provisions.*

*Amen*

# ABOUT THE AUTHOR

Jennifer Farley is a mother, an accomplished educator, and widow who writes with heartfelt honesty and a deep desire to make others feel seen, supported, and less alone. Raised in Oklahoma, Jennifer earned her bachelor's degree in Elementary Education from Langston University and went on to receive a Master of Education with an emphasis in Corporate Wellness from Northcentral University. She has written for the Hope for Widows Foundation, Tulsa Moms, and was featured on the A Frayed Knot podcast.

When she's not writing, Jennifer is often chasing after her three incredible sons, wrangling four energetic dogs, or exploring her love for vintage treasures, gardening, live music, and the occasional (but always enthusiastic) sewing project. She's an avid reader, bird nerd, a hopeful new golfer—even if it means hunting for more lost balls than she finds—and someone who believes in the power of connection through shared stories.

## Shane Farley
### JULY 26, 1973 – APRIL 27, 2015